REAL PROSPERITY

Real Prosperity

*Using the Power of Intuition to Create
Financial and Spiritual Abundance*

Lynn A. Robinson

**Andrews McMeel
Publishing**

Kansas City

04 05 06 07 08 RR4 10 9 8 7 6 5 4 3 2 1

Library of Congress Cataloging-in-Publication Data

Robinson, Lynn A.
    Real prosperity : using the power of intuition to create
financial and spiritual abundance / Lynn A. Robinson.
      p. cm.
    ISBN 0-7407-4201-9
    1. Wealth—Religious aspects—Christianity. 2. Finance,
Personal—Religious aspects—Christianity. I. Title.
BR115.W4R63 2004
204'4—dc22
                                 2004047734

Book design and composition by
Kelly & Company, Lee's Summit, Missouri

This book is dedicated to my husband, Gary,

my soul mate and abundance buddy.

Life is rich beyond measure with you by my side.

Contents

Contents

Acknowledgments

MANY PEOPLE BESIDES THE AUTHOR CONTRIBUTE TO A BOOK. I FEEL richly blessed by wonderful friends and colleagues who have helped me along the path to the creation of a successful career and a life I love. They are:

My husband, Gary. Thank you for your warm heart, quick mind, big soul, and hearty laugh. It's so much fun dreaming big dreams with you.

My stepson Cliff. You have grown into a kind, sensitive, and bright young man. I'm very proud of you. Continue to trust your heart and follow your path.

Laura Straus. Dear friend and soul sister, who always has an encouraging word. I feel abundantly blessed by your support, love, and belief in me.

Barbara Selwyn. I can't believe we've known each other for so long! How did I get to be so lucky to have a friend like you who loves to laugh and enjoy life?

Shane Bowlin. You've been my assistant since my first book. Can you believe we're on number five?! You keep me sane, help me keep my personal and business lives on track and make me laugh at myself. No small feat!

Alison Hendren, coach extraordinaire. What would I have done without you? You are unfailing in your support and have a wonderful sense of humor; you consistently encourage me to move beyond my comfort zone. Thank you from the top of my soul and the bottom of my heart.

My wonderful agent, John Willig. Your enthusiasm, responsiveness, insight, and sense of humor make you a joy to work with.

My terrific friends and colleagues, Lynn Alexander, Bob and Gail Beck, Savita and Michael Brewer, Anne Gilman, John Holland, Shiri Hughes, Karen Foster, Leslie LaRocca, Gail McMeekin, Jean Redpath, Simon Steel, Mark and Beth Sullivan, Jill Winicki, and so many others. Thank you for being there.

To my National Speakers Association buddies, Bob Arnold, Rick Brenner, Barbara Callan-Bogia, Marilee Driscoll, Debbie Hoffman, Mary Marcdante, Nancy Michaels, Diane Ripstein, and Steve Shama. Many thanks for your enthusiasm for life.

To the lovely ladies of the monthly Prosperity Meditation Group, Susan Granata, Lee Rachel Jurman, Elizabeth Meyer, Christiane Perrin, and Roberta Robinson. Thanks for sharing your "abundance energy" with me!

Jean Lucas, my editor—thank you for both championing and editing this book. I appreciate your faith in me as an author.

Thank you also to my clients. This book is the result of thousands of personal conversations over my twenty-year career. It's a tribute to all of you who have listened to your inner voice, trusted its guidance, and had the courage to take action on its wisdom. My heartfelt gratitude to all of you who have shared your joys, pain, and triumphs. You have been wonderful teachers to me.

Introduction

When you follow your heart, when you discover what is truly nourishing to your soul, an abundant, joyful life is just around the corner.

RICHARD CARLSON

I HAVE ALWAYS BEEN FASCINATED BY THE FACT THAT SOME PEOPLE seem to create abundance and success in their lives and others seem to attract only failure and poverty. Is it fate? Are there a lucky few who are destined to have money, fame, and fortune?

Over the past twenty years I've had the privilege of working with thousands of people as a counselor/intuition consultant. I talk with individuals all over the world to help them uncover their goals, visions, and dreams. I encourage them to listen to and trust their intuition—their inner compass—that can point the way to success and prosperity.

I've spoken with individuals who grew up with abuse and poverty, yet went on to experience prosperity and happiness as adults. I've also heard from those who were born with the proverbial "silver spoon," and despite everything they had growing up, many of them feel like failures and have no hope of achieving anything worthwhile.

I wrote *Real Prosperity* because I believe each of us has been given all the resources we need to accomplish the mission we came here to fulfill. We learn to create abundance in our lives and our world through the power of our thoughts and the connection of our Spirit. Many of us have not only forgotten our life purpose, we have also forgotten how to use the tools that forge the path to prosperity, success, love, and health.

There are three premises for this book:

You were born with an inner wisdom called intuition. This is your connection with the Universe, Spirit, Soul, Divine Intelligence, or whatever you choose to call God. When you trust it and follow its guidance it will unfailingly lead to abundance and a joyful life.

The images that you hold in your mind, the strong emotions that you feel, together with your thoughts and beliefs, combine to form a powerful energy that creates your life experience.

There is a Divine flow of abundance through you and all around you. You deserve to have a happy, successful, prosperous life. You cut yourself off from this flow through fear, worry, and animosity. You can learn to stand in this powerful stream of light through love, compassion, service, gratitude, trust, and faith.

I started studying prosperity principles in my mid-twenties when I had five thousand dollars in credit card debt. (An enormous amount at the time.) I had been out of work for months and was now homeless. I was sleeping on a friend's couch at night while desperately looking for a job during the day. Fear, anxiety, and worry consumed me. I remember praying to God for a job, any job.

During one of those desperate entreaties I heard a small, yet distinct, inner voice say, "There is abundance all around you.

Ask for what you truly want." There was a wealth of information in those two sentences. The combined thought that God really heard my prayers and that I could have something more than just a job to pay the bills overwhelmed me. I promptly burst into tears. The fear I'd been living with was miraculously replaced by a calm inner knowing that I was safe and protected, and that everything was going to be okay.

It never occurred to me that I needed to define what I really wanted in life. I simply took what life offered. After this prayer experience I felt as if a veil of illusion had been lifted. I bought a small notebook and began writing down the details of my ideal next job. Two days later I saw a help wanted ad in the paper that caught my attention. However, nothing about it seemed to relate to the description I had written in my journal. My logical mind wanted to disregard it yet I felt a strong inner nudge to send a résumé.

Much to my delight, I received a call to come in for an interview. When I got to the company they informed me that the position I'd applied for was filled. I was momentarily crestfallen until they informed me that another job request had just come in and they thought I might be a good candidate. The job description matched exactly what I had written in my journal. I was hired that day.

This experience taught me that the Universe conspires with us to help achieve our life purpose. There is a Divine plan. Intuition connects us to All-That-Is. This guidance communicates the path of least resistance and helps us accomplish our life's work. I learned during that difficult time in my own life that we live in an abundant world. Unfortunately, we sometimes cut ourselves off from this abundance through fear, worry, and lack of trust.

Since that occurrence almost twenty-five years ago, I've experienced many more miracles and used these as springboards to create both a work life and personal life that I love. I've seen these principles work time and time again in both my own life as well as thousands of others. My stories and their stories are shared in this book.

My passion is to assist you in discovering your own life purpose through connecting with your wise inner guidance system. This book holds the secrets to true prosperity that I've learned through the years. These ideas are introduced in a practical form so you can use them to find your own Divine path to a rich and abundant life.

CHAPTER 1

What Does Prosperity Mean to You?

Success and prosperity now certainly include a balanced life: performing satisfying work while maintaining fitness and health, having loving relationships and a happy family life, being involved in social activities and causes and having a sense of inner peace and fulfillment.

MARK FISHER

WHAT IS PROSPERITY? WOULD YOU BE PROSPEROUS IF YOU HAD five hundred thousand dollars in the bank? Would you consider someone affluent if she had five million dollars? Is your neighbor who drives the late-model Mercedes fabulously rich? You may be surprised to learn that the vast majority of the world population considers *you* truly wealthy simply because you have a roof over your head, clothes on your back, and food on your table. So—why don't you feel prosperous?

The word *prosperity* stems from the Latin root that means "to have hope, success, and good fortune." Others have translated the word more literally as "to go forward hopefully." To be prosperous implies that you have more than enough of what you need and want in life. However, prosperity is not so much a specific dollar amount as an attitude toward life. I believe we live in an abundant world, but how do you begin to learn to tap into the riches? That's what this book is all about.

Wealth is the consciousness of abundance.
And poverty is the consciousness of lack.
Wealth and poverty are both states of mind.

J. DONALD WALTERS

The unfortunate comment I hear most frequently from my clients is, "If I only had the money I would . . ." "live my dreams" . . . "follow my heart" . . . "do the work I love" . . . "make a contribution to the world". . . . If this sounds like you, I ask that you have confidence in yourself as well as in your dream. You have a purpose in life. God would not have instilled this passion and then neglected to give you the means to carry it out. Begin to tune into your own inner wisdom by asking, "How shall I begin?" "What do I need to know?" Be open to receive the answers that will direct you on your path to prosperity.

As you read *Real Prosperity* understand and experience the power you have that will enable you to live a prosperous life. I ask that you approach the philosophy in this book with an open mind. As you read each chapter my hope is that you'll apply the exercises to your own life and refocus your thoughts and emo-

tions from worry and fear to faith, trust, and optimism. I have
seen it work in my own life and those of my clients and students.
I know that you too can reap the harvest and create a prosperous
life you love.

As you continue to read you'll learn to:

Listen to your inner prosperity guide—your intuition—as
it tells you how to create abundance.

Understand the power of positive emotions.

Achieve true security.

Focus on an attitude of gratitude to attract success.

Find freedom from worry, lack, and fear.

Discover your spiritual life mission.

Turn around financial adversity.

Transform your beliefs.

Work with the flow of life to create your heart's desire.

Allow Divine intuition to guide you in small steps to
create positive changes in your spiritual, personal, and
financial life.

Stop self-sabotaging behavior and open the doors to
abundance.

You have an inner dialogue that constantly defines and articu-
lates your view of reality. Are you aware of the things you say to
yourself about money, success, and your ability to create a prosperous life? One of the primary ways to attract the prosperity

you desire is by first becoming aware of your thoughts and attitudes about money. What are some of the things you've been saying to yourself as you have read this chapter?

Your inner chatter interprets events that happen to you through the filter of your beliefs. What many people hear is often very negative or pessimistic. Following are some of the statements I've heard my clients and students make. Do any of them sound familiar?

"I'm so bad with money. It just burns a hole in my pocket."

"Money is the root of all evil."

"I can't make ends meet."

"I'll never be rich."

"You can't be spiritual and have money."

"It's impossible to get ahead in this economy."

"Rich people are bad and take advantage of others."

"I'm so far in debt, I'll never climb out."

"My friends won't like me if I have a lot of money."

"There isn't enough to go around."

"Life is meant to be a struggle."

These conversations you have with yourself are critical because they play a major role in the way you define your reality and thus what you attract to your life experience. You're not stuck with this. Beliefs are something you choose. You can change them and thus begin to change your life and your openness to abundance. By becoming aware of your beliefs and challenging some of the negative assumptions you've made, you begin the process of creating prosperity.

As you continue to read this book, you may find it helpful to create a "prosperity journal" to write down your thoughts as well as your successes as you continue to work with the material. Here are some helpful questions to ask yourself as a way of uncovering your own beliefs about money.

What is your definition of prosperity?

What do you think of people who are wealthy?

What do you think of people who are poor?

What would your life look like if you were prosperous?

What would be the first thing you would change about your life if you were suddenly rich?

Here's a very simple meditation to get you started. It takes just a minute or you can do it for longer if you want. You'll find it quite effective when you're feeling anxious and worried.

Close your eyes, take a deep breath, and say the word "relax" as you slowly let your breath out. Do this several times until you feel yourself becoming calm and centered. Now, simply use the power of your imagination to envision opening to abundance. There is no "right way" to do this. However you experience it is just fine. Quiet your thoughts, let go of any anxious feelings, and draw in a sense of calm, peace, and plenty. Take in this stillness with your inhalation. Let go of any concerns with your exhalation.

***

Expand your feelings of gratitude and appreciation for all that you now have in your life. Say to yourself, "I am filled and surrounded by abundance." Visualize a loving presence enfolding you. Feel yourself open to this presence. Imagine that you are simply sitting in this energy and resting. When you feel ready, open your eyes.

You are prosperous to the degree that you are experiencing peace, health, and plenty in your world.

CATHERINE PONDER

Meditating on abundance a few times a day will produce amazing results. You'll find that it helps you release the fears and worries that are sure to slow down your natural flow of prosperity. Intuitive insights and ideas may pop into your mind after doing this meditation or they may come later in the day while you're driving home from work or making dinner.

Knowing how to create a prosperous life doesn't imply that everything you wish for is instantly manifested. There is a duality of existence that is a bit tricky to master at first. You feel thankful for all that you have. You see abundance around you and focus on it with an attitude of gratitude. However, you also understand that you are constantly growing, learning, and mastering your world. It is natural for you to want more, to have new goals and want to move in different directions.

The Universe is on your side. It wants you to succeed. When you step into the flow of abundance and accept it as your birthright amazing things will begin to occur. Eric Butterworth, author of the book *Spiritual Economics,* writes about it this way, "When you get yourself centered in the universal flow, you become synchronized with this divine bias for good. Amazing things can and will unfold." Bags of gold will not necessarily show up on your doorstep and you may not win the lottery. But synchronicity, coincidences, and miracles directing you to prosperity-producing ideas and associations will become a regular part of your life. Abundance is your natural state. This book will help you discover this truth for yourself and assist you in unfolding the richness of living a life you love.

CHAPTER 2

Abundance Is Your Divine Birthright

*Infinite Mind will put ideas into your mind, words into
your mouth, creativity into your hands, boundless opportunity before you, and guiding light on your way.*

ERIC BUTTERWORTH

STOP FOR A MOMENT AND LOOK AROUND YOU. LOOK AT THE ABUN-
dance that is there before you. I don't necessarily mean all your
material possessions, but look at the trees, clouds, birds, stars,
grass, and flowers. Wherever you are you will see an abundance
of something. We live in an abundant Universe. Money, and the
resources we need to accomplish our life mission, are here in
abundance as well.

Take a slow, deep breath. Feel the air come into your lungs.
Now exhale slowly. It has probably never occurred to you to
worry about whether there is enough air for you to breathe. You
just simply accept that it's there.

You didn't get up one morning, run outside, and begin inhal-
ing like crazy trying to suck up all the air you could for fear that

it would soon be gone. You're not afraid that just because you had air last month the supply will run out and you may not have any next month. Air exists all around you. It flows through your body regardless of whether you feel worthy, have low self-esteem, or experience a rotten childhood. Real prosperity is like that too; you have an abundance of what you need all around you.

You may be thinking, "Yeah, right! You haven't looked at my credit card bills lately. All I see is an abundance of debt!" I know how that feels. I've been there, and when I was, I found this "prosperity-consciousness" talk very irritating. But try out some of the ideas, theories, and principles with an open mind and see where they take you. Someone once said, "If you always do what you've always done, you'll always get what you've always gotten." So, if what you've been doing isn't working, what have you got to lose?

. . . grant that I may become beautiful in my soul within, and that all my external possessions may be in harmony with my inner self.

PLATO

I used to think that if I said my prosperity affirmations fifty times a day and visualized my goals for ten minutes at a time then a pot of gold would appear before me. My other fantasy was that Ed McMahon from Publishers Clearing House would show up at my door announcing I was the latest winner. I have to report that none of those things has happened! But I did come up with a winning lottery number once!

How then do I explain the belief that abundance is all around you? Consider where your prosperity comes from. On the surface you might agree that it comes from your employer or it comes from your clients if you're self-employed. But the thing that enabled you to receive this money was from your ideas, thoughts, intuitions, and feelings about what you wanted to do with your life and how you wanted to make a living.

The ideas and the actions you took on their behalf are your true currency. You acted on an interest that you had and pursued that interest by going to school or learning about it in some other way. You may have had a brilliant idea or an intuitive message that enabled you to create something new or to pursue an entrepreneurial venture. Perhaps you had a hunch that allowed you to simply be at the right place at the right time to get the job you wanted.

Ralph Waldo Emerson wrote, "Man was born to be rich or inevitably to grow rich through the use of his faculties." You may pray for money to pay off your debts or to buy the home of your dreams. However, God doesn't usually swoop in and make a deposit to your bank account. Instead you are given Divine ideas, circumstances, and nudges to move in the direction that allows you to create your dreams.

When you have your mind tuned to the prosperity channel, the intelligence and wisdom of the Universe will begin to broadcast the information you need in order to attract what you are focused upon. What's your choice? Would you rather have your receiver tuned to fear, anxiety, and worry and receive that broadcast? Or would you prefer to profit from the wealth of information that points you toward prosperity when you focus on abundance, gratitude, and hope?

I have a client whom I'll call Ken. He is a practicing Christian and goes to church every Sunday. He told me that he has been praying for years for guidance on how to get out of debt. He shook his head sadly, saying, "God has not answered my prayers." He talked for a while about how unhappy he was in his current business and that he was longing for a change. When he discussed his hopes of one day going into business for himself, his whole energy shifted. He sat upright and spoke in an animated fashion for the first time.

Behold the fowls of the air: for they sow not,
neither do they reap, nor gather into barns;
yet your heavenly Father feedeth them.

MATTHEW 6:26

I asked Ken what stopped him from beginning his business. He answered that until God answered his prayer for more money he didn't feel he could leave his present position. "Ken, is it possible for you to consider that your enthusiasm for your new business idea is one of the ways God is giving you direction toward the prosperity you seek?" I could see from the look on his face that this thought had never crossed his mind. The rest of the session we spent on creating an action plan of small steps he could take to start his new venture.

The word *enthusiasm* comes from the Greek root *entheos*. It literally means "God within." Ken's excitement about his new business concept was part of the answer to his prayer and he responded to the Divine ideas that were filling his mind. When last I heard from Ken he was making five hundred thousand dollars a year and feeling considerably more prosperous.

Remember when you were a kid and saw a falling star? Someone was sure to have said, "Make a wish!" That's what I want you to do right now. What would your ideal life look like? Get out a big piece of paper or a notebook and begin to write and/or draw what you want. *Note:* Do not concern yourself at this point about how you will achieve these goals. Your assignment right now is to stretch your unused muscles of imagination and begin to dream. The purpose is to give a clear message to the Universe about what you want. In the next chapters we'll work on all the ways you might receive the replies that the Universe sends!

Things to write/dream/draw about to get you started:

What does your home look like? Who are your friends? What do you do for fun? How much money would you like to have? Describe how you want to look and feel. What kind of primary relationship would you like (if any)? What kind of work are you doing? Describe your ideal relationship with your family. What do your surroundings look like? Do you want to travel? If so, where? How do you feel about your spiritual life?

Think of five times in your life where money, money-making ideas, or resources came to you unexpectedly. Write about them in your prosperity journal. When you've completed the exercise, ask yourself what you have learned by writing about these situations.

One of the secrets of creating prosperity is to fully use the capacity of your imagination to vividly picture and experience what it's like to be a person of affluence. This is what people refer to when they say someone has a "prosperity consciousness." When you have this awareness you know in the core of your being that you deserve and easily create whatever you need and want. Dare to dream big. See yourself as capable, gifted, and successful. You are! Then begin to move confidently in the direction of your dreams. That's what you were put on Earth to do.

CHAPTER 3

See Your Life as You Want It to Be

The trouble with many plans is that they are based on the way things are now. To be successful, your personal plan must focus on what you want, not what you have.

NIDO QUBEIN

WHAT WOULD YOUR IDEAL LIFE LOOK LIKE? WOULD YOU BE A WORLD traveler? Have a big house on acres of land? Would you be a philanthropist and give your abundance to worthy people and causes? Perhaps you yearn for simpler things, a small, cozy house with room in the yard for your garden, the financial resources to stay home and parent your kids, or the extra money to help out your parents in their old age. Each of us has different goals, but we have one thing in common—what we hold in our mind and feel in our heart are created in our life.

Many of you know that your thoughts and beliefs are considered important in creating what you want in life. I'm going to add another piece to the equation that I think is equally, if not more, important—your emotions. I am not a physicist, so here's a layperson's understanding of how energy works.

Your feelings and emotions are full of energy that will either attract or repel what you want. For example, when you imagine yourself getting that promotion you've been seeking, you feel excited, buzzed, hopeful, and upbeat. Your positive feelings are full of vibrational waves that are magnetically charged and will begin to attract the circumstances reflected in your predominant emotion. When you have a strong intent or goal it's as if a ray of energy goes out to the Universe, projected by your emotions. This energy begins to attract you to the object of your focus.

Broke is temporary. Poor is eternal.

ROBERT KIYOSAKI

You picked up this book presumably because you wanted to experience more prosperity in your life. When you're feeling optimistic about money your primary feelings are up—confident, high-frequency vibrations that will attract prosperity to you. It might help to imagine your emotions and thoughts as magnets. If you dwell on positive emotions about money and abundance you will begin to magnetize or attract that which you desire.

Conversely, if you're always worried, full of fear and anxiety, and spend a lot of time each day focusing your emotions and attention on how poor you are, you're broadcasting your poverty.

These emotions create low-frequency vibrations and will begin to draw to you many of the things you fear. You may be spending time in meditation actively affirming, "I have an abundance of money," and yet be largely focused on your feelings of dread about the hopelessness of coming up with enough money for the next car payment.

Fortunately, you don't manifest the focus of thoughts and feelings instantly! Throughout any given day you probably have your share of positive feelings along with some negative ones. Your thoughts put into motion what you ultimately create. Your emotions energize those thoughts. The stronger your emotion, the faster you'll magnetize what you're focusing on.

Your emotions are a powerful communication conduit from your intuition. When you experience strong negative emotions, pay attention! Your inner guidance is trying to tell you something. "You are moving away from your goals." It's not possible to feel angry, bitter, and fearful, and at the same time be in harmony with what you want to create. Those emotions just push your goals away.

I had a client who was fixated on not thinking negatively. Talking to her was often quite comical. She would say, "Ohmygosh! I had another negative thought!" Then she would wave her hand over her head and say, "Cancel! Cancel!" as if to thwart the potential consequences of her contrary thoughts!

Breaking the pattern of thinking negatively and feeling negative emotions is just a matter of habit. It doesn't require constant vigilance or scolding yourself! Have a relaxed attitude about it. When you notice your mind straying to something you don't want, stop, smile, and gently bring your focus back to what you do want.

I don't want you to believe that unless you're thinking like Pollyanna or whistling, "Don't Worry, Be Happy!" all day that you're hopeless on the prosperity front. On the contrary, you're beginning to pay attention to the valuable resource of your inner guidance. In the next few chapters you'll learn some helpful and practical tools to shift the focus of your emotions and begin to create the abundance you desire.

I've been rich and I've been poor.
Believe me, honey, rich is better!

SOPHIE TUCKER

Here are the basic steps you use to create anything in life:

Decide what you don't want. You might find yourself saying things like: "I'm not challenged by this job any longer." Or "I'm sick of being broke." Or "I can't keep putting all this money into fixing my old car." Or "I'm not happy in this relationship any longer." When you find yourself becoming drained, bored, exhausted, enervated, or depleted by anything or anyone it's a message from your intuition that a change is needed.

Decide what you do want. You may not know the specific job you want or exactly what to do about the relationship that's creating unhappiness. Begin to play around with the idea of creating something new. People rarely know *exactly* what they want. Ask yourself, "What do I feel excited about?" Pay attention to when you hit on something that makes you feel lighter and enthusiastic, or even if you feel just a flicker of interest. This is one way your intuition gives you hints about the direction you need to follow.

—◦◦◦◦—

Do what you love, and the money will follow.

MARSHA SINETAR

—◦◦◦◦—

Pump up the volume of positive emotion. Spend time each day daydreaming about your life and what it will be like to achieve your goals. Your strong, positive feelings have the power to attract your desires. If a new job is your goal, you might imagine all the aspects of your new job and how great you'll feel. You may imagine what you'll do with the additional money that the new position will likely bring. You could imagine the new friends and colleagues you'll have in your new job and how well you work as a team. Keep your focus on whatever makes you feel good about attaining your desire. I call this *flowing the energy.*

Pay attention to your intuition. Begin to expect the manifestation of your goals. Act as if they will happen and pay attention to your intuition. When you have your mind and emotions firmly focused on your hopes and dreams, your intuition will begin to give you guidance to the next steps. This wisdom may come through your gut feelings, inner voice, dreams, a sense of knowing, or even a physical sensation. You may begin to experience coincidences and synchronicities. That's how you'll know you're on the right track.

Be willing to dream big. Ask for a lot. Take a risk and go for what you want the most in your life. Most of us think too small and drown ourselves and our desires with thoughts that begin with "I can't," "I shouldn't," "I don't deserve it," or "It's not possible." The power of the Universe wants to flow through you to create everything you need and wish for. When you think too small you block the flow. Don't settle for a little life. There is a wonderful plan for you. Respect that still, small voice inside that is encouraging you forward. That's where the true answers lie.

CHAPTER 4

Listen to Your Inner Millionaire

When we surrender to God, we surrender to something bigger than ourselves—to a universe that knows what it's doing. When we stop trying to control events they fall into a natural order, an order that works. We're at rest while a power much greater than our own takes over, and it does a much better job than we could have done. We learn to trust that the power that holds galaxies together can handle the circumstance of our relatively little lives.

MARIANNE WILLIAMSON

WOULDN'T IT BE WONDERFUL TO HAVE AN ALL-KNOWING GUIDE in your life that could help you make the right choices to create a prosperous and successful life? You do! It's called your intuition. When you pay attention and listen to its wisdom it will connect you with a greater knowledge. You may call that knowledge God/Goddess, All That Is, Divine Intelligence, the Universe, Higher Wisdom, or any other name/concept that works for you.

It's the part of you that has an overview of your life and knows what you need in order to create the life you were born to live.

My friend Jean Redpath is a Scottish singer. She told me a story when, as a young and starving artist, she went on a shopping trip with friends in Liverpool and fell in love with a particularly beautiful evening gown. She was singing in funky folk clubs at the time and struggled for days with the ridiculous idea of the gown. "What was I going to do with an evening gown? And, good heavens, how could I afford it?!" Nonetheless, the impulse persisted and when Jean discovered that it was on sale at a 70 percent discount, she swallowed hard and bought the gorgeous gown that she described as a lovely "Middle Ages green," replete with lace and ruffles. Several weeks later she received an invitation from the royal family, requesting her to sing before the queen in the banqueting hall of Edinburgh Castle. In that setting, the dress was perfect!

Intuition has been described as "I know, but I don't know how I know." Sometimes you don't even know what you know! Jean's inner prosperity guide was prompting her with visions of singing before multitudes, and for that she'd need a gown. It didn't necessarily communicate that Queen Elizabeth would be requesting her presence at the royal court. However, Jean heeded her inner promptings to purchase a seemingly unneeded gown and was prepared when she received the career-making request from the queen.

I had a somewhat less dramatic situation happen to me. When I first began doing intuitive readings for a living, I was subletting an office a few days a week from a colleague. This arrangement seemed to be working fine. However, one morning I woke up with a strong desire to increase the number of days I was renting the office and to complete and print a large quantity of new brochures. This made no logical sense. I didn't need more brochures or more office time. Nevertheless, I was not one to quibble with my inner guidance, so I set about doing what my intuition suggested. Several weeks later I learned that I had been voted "Best Psychic" by readers of *Boston* magazine. I was swamped with clients and requests for my brochure.

How and why do the above examples happen? I believe that when you hold a strong vision of what you want, you're sending a positive energy (your feelings and emotions) toward this goal. The universal Law of Attraction works like this: You feel a strong emotion that sets up a vibration of sorts. Through this energy you begin to magnetize circumstances and conditions that will allow you to create your desire.

Divine intuition begins to send messages to you to help you find the right path and to assist you in making the correct choices. Synchronicities and coincidences begin to occur. You may feel drawn to just the right person who will help you with your business idea. Your intuition may also take the form of a gut feeling about a certain stock to invest in, a dream about a new invention you'll have a hand in creating, or an idea about a marketing plan for your company. You take action based on your inner guidance, and as you follow your inner promptings and enthusiasms, you begin to attract and create your goal.

It's also important to pay attention to occasions when you feel resistant to doing something. It's not always procrastination. It may be your intuition warning you not to take an action that will deplete your prosperity. Your inner guidance is a compass of your soul. It will point you in the direction of success by giving you feelings of excitement and enthusiasm for a particular course of action. It will also provide the proverbial pit in the bottom of your stomach, the gut feeling that leads you away from a potential disaster. Often we dismiss these feelings, sensations, and "knowings" at our peril.

Our desires are the way in which our soul guides us along our path in life.

SHAKTI GAWAIN

I had a recent example of this happen to me. My previous book, *Divine Intuition,* had just come out and I was quite excited about promoting it. However, eight weeks after the book was in the stores I found myself feeling uncharacteristically tired whenever I tried to do anything involved with the promotion. It turned out that the book sold out within two months and there was a lag time of three months before it would be in stores again. If I had fought my resistance and continued to promote it during that time, it would have been a huge waste of energy and money.

I'm often amazed at how the Universe works when we pay attention to our inner guidance and choose to trust. Several years ago I received a call from a literary agent who asked if I'd be interested in coauthoring a book in the *Complete Idiot's Guide* series. She gave me a very short time deadline—twelve weeks to finish a four hundred–plus-page manuscript, working with a coauthor I hadn't met. She also stated apologetically that she could offer only a very small advance.

I meditated on this offer for a day or so. It would mean virtually closing down my intuitive consulting business for three months to work on this project. I was nervous about it because it would be a significant loss of income. Despite my concerns, I knew I should say yes. I felt strongly that it would all work out and that somehow the money would come from another source.

Ideas are like seeds; when they first come up you don't know what they're going to grow into. Just keep following your joyful impulses, and your ideas will unfold into the forms that best serve you.

SANAYA ROMAN

I called the agent and said I would do it. The very afternoon I said yes to the book, my husband called to say that he'd received a large contract that provided us with enough money to more than make up for my diminished income. I hasten to add that the Universe doesn't always act *that* quickly to bring prosperity but it gave me a huge boost of faith that I had made the right decision and that my "inner millionaire" was hard at work.

Begin to put your inner millionaire to work! Come up with a list of questions that you'd like some help with. Examples might be, "I want work that is creative, fun, and will allow me to make $___ a year or more. What steps should I take?" Or, "What's the best thing I could do to allow more prosperity into my life?" Whenever one of these questions comes to mind, simply close your eyes, take several deep breaths, and relax into stillness. Pose your question and listen quietly for the answer. If it doesn't come immediately to mind, don't worry. The answer will probably pop into your mind when you least expect it.

You deserve to have a prosperous and abundant life. You have within you a rich inner-guidance system that will constantly direct you by encouraging you to do what you love. The money that you seek will come much more quickly if you are focused on making decisions based on joy and passion instead of doing things that make you feel exhausted, depleted, or compromised.

As you begin to follow your inner-prosperity guide you'll find things happening quickly and easily. Miracles and coincidences will occur and you'll discover yourself becoming one of those people who are in the right place at the right time. Others may think you're merely lucky. But you'll know the truth. You've got a hotline to prosperity—your intuition!

CHAPTER 5

Create a Positive Financial Statement

*When it comes to your money, what you think will direct
what you say, what you say will direct what you do,
and what you do will create your destiny.*

SUZE ORMAN

ALL OF US HAVE AN INNER DIALOGUE THAT BABBLES TO US DURING our waking moments. It says things like, "The economy is so bad it's going to be tough getting a job." Or, "I wish I had more money. I'll probably never be rich." It is constantly judging, perceiving, and commenting. It interprets events that happen to us through the filter of our beliefs. Unfortunately for many of us, this inner chatter is often very negative or pessimistic. What do you say to yourself about money and your ability to achieve a prosperous life?

If you could have read my mind during my pre-prosperity days, you would have heard, "I never seem to have any money." "I hope the brakes hold out on my car for another few weeks. How will I afford to fix them? I'll need new tires soon." "Why can't I seem to get ahead? How much have I saved toward my rent payment this month? It's probably not enough." "I'd love to have a new dress for Jane's party but my credit card is maxed out. I guess I'll have to wear that old one." You get the idea.

If you accept that your thoughts create reality, you can see what mine were creating! In fact, I used to joke that the Universe seemed to know when I had a few bucks in my pocket because as soon as I began to feel the least bit abundant a crisis would occur and the money would disappear.

I learned about affirmations during this time. Affirmations are one of the primary ways that we can begin to control the shaping of our thoughts and attitudes in order to create change in our lives. When we affirm what we want, we make a strong, positive statement about something we wish to take place in our life.

I worked on those affirmations diligently. I wrote them down in a journal several times a day and said them to myself during meditations at night. I recently reread some of those journals where I had written, "I now have a million dollars." "I am prosperous." "I am a magnet to money." I realize now why they didn't work at the time. I was spending every other waking minute affirming the opposite through my inner dialogue.

You can't swing from "How will I pay the rent?" to "I easily attract money" and expect any kind of positive transformation. You must begin to change your inner dialogue.

Every thought you think has an energy or vibration. If you really want something (prosperity) and hold positive thoughts and feelings about it, you will attract it into your life. If you really *don't* want something (poverty) and constantly feel fear and anxiety about it, you will attract it into your life. Whatever you put your focus on begins a process of manifestation. Think about something—positive or negative—with enough strong intent and emotion and you will have it in your life.

The interesting thing about holding strong beliefs about anything is that you'll see proof of your convictions everywhere. If your focus is on fear of losing money, you will find yourself drawn to the news reports about the poor economy, bankruptcies, lay-offs, and the downward spiral of the stock market. You will also be surrounded by people who have a victim mentality and who agree with you that the rich get richer and the poor get poorer. "Argue for your limitations and sure enough, they're yours," Richard Bach wrote in his book *Illusions*.

If, on the contrary, your focus is on easily creating abundance, you'll be drawn to the news that a particular sector of the economy is doing well, or that a local company is hiring more employees. Ideas will pop into your mind that will allow you to make more money. You'll also, more often than not, find yourself in the company of people who are financially successful and hold views that agree with yours.

So how do you begin to make this change from worry and anxiety to peace and faith? You must begin to focus on your heart's desire rather than on your worst fears. Does it happen overnight? Probably not. Can you begin today? Yes.

Make a commitment right now to pay attention to what you tell yourself. When you find yourself feeling anxious or scared about your financial situation—slow down, pay attention, stop. Begin to notice the thoughts that preceded your fear. What were you focusing on just before the apprehension began? More than likely, you were dwelling on ideas of a fearful event, not being able to pay your bills, your car breaking down, or being out on the street. Is this what you want to create in your life? No? Then it's time to begin to break the habit of those thoughts. That's all they are, a habit. Habits can be broken and changed. In the book *A Course in Miracles,* Dr. Helen Schucman states, "I can choose peace instead of this." That's what you need to do to begin. Make a conscious choice to choose peaceful (and prosperous) thoughts.

We heal ourselves on the mental level as we become aware of our core beliefs, release those that limit us, and open to more supportive ideas and greater understanding.

SHAKTI GAWAIN

Many people have told me that they're just "anxiety prone." I believe that in many cases your anxiety stems from what you're telling yourself. Try a simple experiment. Close your eyes and say the following to yourself for about thirty to sixty seconds. "I'll never get ahead. I'm really a failure. I'll always be in debt." How do you feel? Depressed? Demoralized? Anxious? Hopeless? It's virtually impossible to take any kind of positive action to get yourself out of poverty if you believe these things.

Now do the same experiment and focus on these statements: "Things will work out." "I'm learning about prosperity and things are beginning to change for me." "Today I'll take some steps that will open up some opportunities for more income." Now how do you feel? Hopeful? Optimistic? More confident? When you're in this state it's much easier for you to be open to intuitive messages pointing you to avenues of prosperity.

The key is to choose thoughts that make you feel better. In the previous paragraph I wasn't asking you to affirm something like, "I'm rich." Or, "I have all the money I need." Your mind would have simply replied, "Yeah, right! Have you seen my latest bank balance?!" The statements I chose were what I call "bridge beliefs." They were simply statements that didn't have a strong positive or negative charge but allowed you to feel better and thus more open to your intuition.

Changing your negative thinking is like breaking any bad habit. It happens in stages. The first step is to be clear about what you don't want. For example, "I don't want to be in debt." "I don't want to worry about paying my bills." Then, state clearly what you do want. For example, "I want to experience prosperity in all areas of my life." "I want to feel ease and flow about the subject of money." From now on when you find yourself having a negative thought or beginning to worry or feel anxious, replace it with a thought that feels better.

Choose a phrase from the list below that resonates with you. It should be a group of words that gives you some relief from your anxiety or that makes you feel empowered in some way. Please feel free to mix and match any of the following or create one of your own.

Money is beginning to flow more easily into my life.

I am open to new avenues of abundance.

Peace, be still.

I choose faith over fear.

God (the Universe) supports me.

I am in the process of positive change regarding prosperity.

My thoughts create my life and I choose positive ones.

My intuition is guiding me with prospering thoughts and ideas.

My life is filled with abundance.

Prosperity is my Divine right.

I choose to focus on abundance.

Everything will work out.

My income is constantly increasing.

My intuition is providing me with ideas for prosperity.

Money and moneymaking ideas flow to me easily.

Money flows freely into my life and I always have enough to meet my needs.

I am open to new avenues for work, money, and creativity.

From now on when you begin to feel worried or anxious—stop. Replace the thought you were thinking with the phrase you've chosen from the previous list.

You cannot worry about your bills and focus on abundance at the same time. Choose the thought that uplifts you and points you in the direction you want to go. If you'd like to feel deliciously abundant, read through this excerpt from *The Power of Your Subconscious Mind* by Joseph Murphy.

I like money, I love it, I use it wisely, constructively, and judiciously. Money is constantly circulating in my life. I release it with joy and it returns to me multiplied in a wonderful way. It is good and very good. Money flows to me in avalanches of abundance. I use it for good only, and I am grateful for my good and for the riches of my mind. I am one with the infinite riches of my subconscious mind. Money flows to me copiously, freely, and endlessly. It is my right to be rich, happy, and successful. I am forever conscious of my true worth. I give of my talents freely and I am wonderfully blessed financially. It is wonderful, and so it is.

Watch your manner of speech if you wish to develop a peaceful state of mind. Start each day by affirming peaceful, contented, and happy attitudes and your days will tend to be pleasant and successful.

NORMAN VINCENT PEALE

As you maintain your conscious and deliberate focus on abundance, your world will begin to change. Unexpected sources of money will appear. You'll start to use your inner wisdom to attract new ideas for ways to live fully and successfully. Resources and support will begin to flow into your life. These will give way to action, and before you know it a new life, free of worry and anxiety, will be yours.

CHAPTER 6

Visualize and Live Your Dreams

Creative visualization is magic in the truest and highest meaning of the word. It involves understanding and aligning yourself with the natural principles that govern the workings of our universe, and learning to use these principles in the most conscious and creative way.

SHAKTI GAWAIN

MOST OF YOU HAVE PROBABLY HEARD OF THE POWER OF VISUALI-zation. It's holding a picture in your mind of something you want to achieve. Olympic athletes envision a successful comple-tion of their individual event. Sales people frequently use it to pump themselves up for a meeting with a prospective client. In this chapter I want to show you how the combination of visuali-zation and positive emotion can magnify your ability to make your dreams come true.

Close your eyes for just a moment and simply picture what it would be like to have all the money you need. Do it now.... Feel any emotions that arise and pay attention to the images you receive. Are you alone? If not, who is with you? What time of year is it? What do your surroundings look like? Are you aware of any particular smells, colors, or sounds? Enlarge the image. Think bigger. Again, ask yourself, "What would my life look like if I had all the money I needed?"

Success is the outward manifestation of an inner focus, the result of steering thoughts toward a specific target.

MARK FISHER

When I did that brief exercise, I experienced an intense feeling of security, warmth, love, and peace. The image that came to mind was cooking in an open, light-filled, gourmet kitchen. (I love to cook!) I was looking out over a serene, flower-filled lawn, surrounded by several acres of forest in which birds were singing. A slow-moving stream flowed through the corner of our yard into a lake that I could glimpse out the window. I felt joy that we lived in a lovely and gracious home. My mind shifted momentarily to later in the evening, laughing with close friends who had come to enjoy dinner with us.

That thirty-second visualization defines all of the elements of prosperity for me. It's a snapshot of what a prosperous life looks and feels like. I'm surrounded by nature, a beautiful home, and the resources to create a wonderful meal for my friends and family. Your image is obviously going to be different. It might involve world travel, a home in the city, a new car, or the ability to be a philanthropist or simply to be able to do work you love, or having ample abundance to pay your bills. Whatever you imagined, you took a conscious step toward creating the prosperous life you desire.

You'll read it in the Bible, hear it from people ranging from philosophers to physicists to self-help authors—what you hold in your mind is what you create in your life. The keys are (1) being conscious of what you want to create, and (2) practicing the art of holding positive images or visualizations of the successful completion of your goal.

You may think you've never been successful at this visualization stuff. I maintain you've been extremely successful. How can I say that without knowing you? Look around you. If you see areas of your life where you've been successful, you've achieved those results through the power of the pictures you hold in your mind. Conversely, if you have areas of your life you're not happy with, you've undoubtedly held images that have also affected the outcome. Either way, you've successfully created in your life the images you've held in your mind. Now, which ones do you choose to focus on to create the outcome you desire? That's the important point!

To be honest, there are many factors that create success or failure in our lives. They include all the things you're reading about in this book—positive self-talk, prayer, intuition, visualization, and emotions, to name a few. Your mind's ability to imagine and focus on a desired outcome is one of the most powerful tools at your disposal. All the rest of the techniques and methods will assist you once you have the image of your goal firmly implanted in your mind.

Many other books and chapters in this book have been written on the art of visualization. Most of you know that it's considered important to spend five to fifteen minutes a day visualizing your goals. I believe there is one important component missing from many descriptions of the practice of visualization and that is positive emotion.

Try this:

1. Spend about thirty seconds visualizing your ideal job. Okay. Got it?

2. Now spend thirty seconds visualizing that ideal job and pump it up with feeling. See and feel yourself having fun, enjoying your day. Imagine how terrific it feels to go to work. What are the elements that are fun or enjoyable for you? Imagine the enjoyment of interacting with colleagues who are supportive and appreciative. What do your surroundings look like? Imagine how great you feel in your perfect office. What makes you feel good? Pump up the volume on those feelings. Okay. How do you feel now?

Which of the two techniques above will succeed in generating the right energy for you to magnetize and manifest the work you love? If you chose #2 with its emphasis on strong, positive emotions, you'd be right.

Here's a fun and creative technique to assist you in using the power of your mind to achieve success. Do you remember a time in your life when you felt on top of the world? It might have been a time when you won an award and you took the stage and everyone was cheering for you. Perhaps you gave a recital and did it perfectly and you felt really proud of yourself. Maybe the event was hitting the baseball high over the left field fence and getting the winning run for your team. Whatever it was, write about it in your journal.

Summarize in a sentence what it is you want to create as the next success in your life. Examples might be an ideal job, a prosperous life, a description of your dream home. Whatever it is, write about it in your journal.

Describe three different scenes in which you have what you want. You might want to reread the paragraph at the beginning of the chapter for ideas. My images included a light-filled gourmet kitchen, a beautiful home, and a nature-filled yard. For me, these symbolize the prosperity I desire. Write about your scenes in your journal.

Whatever your mind can conceive and believe,
it can achieve.

NAPOLEON HILL

Choose a piece of music that makes you feel really happy and up. I love to dance, so I always choose dance tunes from the seventies and eighties. Your taste might lean toward classical, jazz, New Age, country, or rhythm and blues. It doesn't matter what kind of music it is as long as it makes your heart soar!

Put on your CD or tape, close your eyes, and combine all the elements in the first three steps. These are: (1) Bring to mind the time you were successful. Spend about thirty seconds imagining and feeling the full emotions of the event, (2) Continue to enjoy those good feelings while you shift your focus to what you want to create, (3) Envision and feel the emotion as you see the successful attainment of your goals. Visualize and feel the three components that you wrote about above. Get into the energy of the music. Dance (or at least move) and allow it to help you expand your good feelings. Spend as much time as you want enjoying this phase of the exercise.

⁓

The game of life is a game of boomerangs.
Our thoughts, deeds, and words return to us
sooner or later, with astounding accuracy.

FLORENCE SCOVEL SHINN

⁓

Whew! Open your eyes and look around the room. You have just ramped up your manifesting and magnetizing energy. Feel good? The life you desire is on its way! All of the insights you gather as you write about and visualize your ideal life come from your intuition communicating to you. Your enthusiasm and excitement mean that the Universe is saying yes to your goals.

CHAPTER 7

Invest in a Prayerful Life

*Prayer is not the overcoming of God's reluctance, but
the taking hold of God's willingness.*

PHILLIP BROOKS

OUR WORLD IS IN A TIME OF GREAT TRANSITION. CORPORATIONS
are downsizing. Jobs once considered secure are being phased
out. You may be one of those people who are beginning to re-
vision your work life and retirement years, and are calling on
your faith and trust in a Universal wisdom to guide you. Meditation and prayer are two important tools to use to focus on a
prosperous and successful life. Your inner guidance will put
thoughts in your mind and opportunity before you as you move
in the direction of your goals.

Someone once said that prayer is when we talk to God and
meditation is when He answers. Prayer connects us to the invisible
intelligence that is wired to our soul. Prayer is asking for help
and wisdom. Philosopher Ralph Waldo Emerson wrote, "Prayer
is the contemplation of the facts of life from the highest point

of view." How do you view prayer and how can you use it to receive the insight and guidance you desire?

I grew up in a Christian household. We weren't particularly religious or spiritual. However, each night before I went to bed I said the prayer that many of you are familiar with: "Now I lay me down to sleep. I pray the Lord my soul to keep. If I should die before I wake, I pray the Lord my soul to take." Now, I don't know about you, but as a kid, that terrified me. Somehow I got it into my little brain that if I didn't pray, God was going to take my soul and I'd die. You would think this might be motivation to pray more! On the contrary, for many years I wanted to avoid prayer altogether and saw God as the enemy who decided whether I would live or die.

Over many years and much inner seeking I came to the realization that God was not the old man on a throne looking down from heaven whom I'd imagined as a child. Instead, I began to feel and experience God as a Universal Wisdom, as Divine Love, and as an energy force that wanted only the best for me. I saw that all of the challenges I was experiencing in life were gifts that God put there to help me find my way "back home."

I learned that when I talked to God, He answered. It wasn't a booming voice out of the clouds. He answered through the still, small voice of my intuition. Each time I struggled with fear, anxiety, anger, or any of the minor and major upsets of life, I learned to ask for help. It wasn't the prayer from my childhood. It was more of a conversation with a good friend.

The answers came in a variety of ways. My problems were not usually "fixed" in the ways that I might have liked. Money did not pour out of the heavens, and so far no one has left me a million dollars in their will! Sometimes the answers would come in a fleeting thought: "Maybe I could try this. . . ." On other occasions I might be drawn to a book that had the answers I was seeking. Many times the answer to my prayers was a boost to my self-confidence when I most needed it.

Pray. Pray. Pray. Loving gifts of thought
and healing will never be wasted.
Prayer is activating your thread to God.

BARBARA MARK AND TRUDY GRISWOLD

Whether your concerns are about paying the rent this month, wrestling with your credit card debt, dealing with a difficult relationship, or struggling with a health crisis, the guidance you receive from prayer can be a balm for your soul. Let God know about whatever is on your mind. It doesn't need to be formal. It's like a conversation with your best friend. Whatever is on your mind matters, however trivial it may seem. Ask for help, for insight, for peace, for strength, or whatever you most deeply desire. You always have access to this inner wisdom, although sometimes it takes practice and silence to learn to listen and understand. Prayer opens your mind to new opportunities. When you pray you are reaching for a Power that is bigger than you.

The very nature of prayer puts you in touch with a wisdom that guides your life. It is the force that created the universe and directs the sun to rise every morning and to set every night. Wouldn't you rather put your faith in this Power to help you resolve your financial issues than in the "little you" of your logical, rational mind? I believe that God sees the totality of who you are and what you are here to learn and knows the most direct way for you to create your heart's desire.

God's direction usually leads you to solutions by taking you by the "Hills of Hope," the "Paths of Patience," the "Lanes of Love," and the "Fields of Faith" as a way to help you in your life crises. Those are the easiest paths to take. Through your own free will you may also choose the "Highway of Hatred," the "Freeway of Fear," or the "Avenue of Anxiety."

Prayer is the one thing that can make a change in your life. It matters not what your religion may be or whether you adhere to none. If you will go direct to God in simple, affirmative prayer, you can heal your body, bring peace and harmony into your life, enlarge your social contacts, and make prosperity a reality.

EMMET FOX

You may not know how to get to the destination called "Prosperity and Abundance." You will need to listen carefully to your inner guidance to be shown the way. My prayer is that you allow hope, patience, love, and faith to guide you there. The choice is yours.

Many clients have told me that they'll have faith when they have enough money and they can finally relax. That's when they'll experience peace, joy, and harmony. My response is that they have it backward. First you make a choice to have faith that all will be well. You begin to understand that there is an abundance of what you need. You believe that you deserve health, prosperity, and love and you open yourself to allowing it into your life. You begin to make choices because you are driven by your inner guidance. You begin to release the idea that you are a victim of your circumstances. Then you begin to trust that if you take one small step followed by another small step, the prosperity will begin to show up in your life. And it will.

We live in a love-based and abundant universe. What you desire in your life can be yours. Part of the lesson plan is to learn to allow this rich bounty by recognizing that you deserve love, healing, and prosperity. There is no virtue in fear and suffering.

I remember a time when I literally didn't have a clue about how to pray. I only knew the prayers from church and childhood, and they didn't bring me true comfort. You may have a different experience. Please do whatever brings you peace and solace and connection with the Divine. However, if you feel you need some help with praying for prosperity, here are some ideas.

1. Prayers don't necessarily need to be formal occasions where you set aside half an hour or more. When you find yourself in an anxious state regarding your finances (or lack thereof) say a brief prayer. Close your eyes and imagine you are in conscious contact with God. Don't worry; you can't do this wrong. Here are some phrases that might help:

"I am open and receptive to new avenues of income."

"Help me to feel at peace about my finances."

"I ask for guidance to bring prosperity into my life."

"Help me to release my fear and to know that I am worthy of abundance."

"I affirm a life of joyful prosperity."

2. When you wake up in the morning, before you go to bed at night, and any time during the day, simply pause to pray. The Universal Wisdom that is God is available in every moment. Feel your Divine connection when you stop for a traffic light or while drinking your morning coffee.

3. Meister Eckhart stated, "If the only prayer you ever say in your entire life is thank you, it will be enough." Say a prayer of thanks each day for all that you *do* have. As you focus on gratitude your life will flow with more abundance.

Still need some help? What are some easy-to-remember phrases that you can say to yourself when you become anxious, fearful, or depressed about money? These might be verses from the Bible, the Koran, a book of prayers, or any other inspirational writing of your choice. Or choose a comforting phrase that one of your parents said to you when you were young. Put the words on a Post-it note and stick it on your wall. You can also write them on a slip of paper and place it in your wallet, your checkbook, or any other place where you'll see it frequently.

When you pray you place your trust in a higher will. You open yourself to the intelligence of the Universe. You are saying in effect, "I don't know what's best for me or how to proceed. Help me understand. Help me become whole." True prayer aligns you with the will of God. If you listen deeply you will hear your directions. It is always a message of love, hope, and yes . . . abundance.

CHAPTER 8

"Help Wanted" Ads to God

When you have learned how to decide with God, all decisions become as easy and as right as breathing. There is no effort, and you will be led as gently as if you were being carried down a quiet path to summer.

HELEN SCHUCMAN

I WANT TO SHARE A TECHNIQUE WITH YOU THAT I'VE BEEN USING for years. I feel it's played a central role in manifesting miracles in my life. I have a box on a shelf in my home office that says "Help Wanted." It sits by a lovely sculpture of a glass angel who watches over it. It contains letters I've sent to God.

As I discussed in the previous chapter, I consider prayer a vital element in allowing abundance into our lives. Prayer is how we talk with God and intuition is one of the ways He answers. I'm a bit of a pragmatist and sometimes I'd wonder if God heard my prayers. So I devised a system that satisfied my need for some sort of a tangible signal that I was sending a communication to God that I wished him to hear and take action on. It works like this:

I write a letter to God telling him about my concerns. I always feel a sense of relief in writing these. It's as if I'm talking with a good friend and sharing my worries. I pour out my fears and anxieties on the page. Then I go a step further. I make specific requests of God to help me in certain ways, always adding, "if this is in my highest interest." Far be it from me to tell God what to do in my life! But I like to think God is interested in helping me with my specific concerns and will assist me in unique ways that I could never have come up with on my own. I figure that the Power that created the Universe and all its inhabitants will certainly know how to assist each of us in an easy and effortless way.

Here's an example of a letter that I wrote to God in 1986 and placed in my "Help Wanted" box.

Dear God,

As you know, I'm the operations manager of a software company. I really appreciate my job and enjoy the people I work with. However, I find that I'm growing restless there and can't help but think there's something else I should be doing for work.

I've been seeing a career counselor for several weeks and I keep coming up with the fact that I love the idea of counseling, and I have a huge interest in metaphysics and intuition. I'm also interested in pursuing a career where I can be self-employed. I took a class in psychic development and found that I was really good at it. Maybe this is something that can combine all my interests?

Requests:

I'd like to have a full-time, successful psychic reading business.
I'd like to attract wonderful people whom I enjoy working with.
I'd like to work in a beautiful and easily affordable office
surrounded by nature.

God, if the above is in my highest interests, please work with me to bring this into my life. Thank you for all Your blessings. I remain open to your guidance and direction.

Amen.

Over the next few weeks I continued my work with the career counselor, who helped me to further define my vocation. I also began a daily plan of visualizing my beautiful office and an appointment book full of wonderful clients. I told one or two friends about my desires. My main concern was "How can I develop such an exotic skill into a business?" I quipped that if God posted a "Psychic Wanted" ad in the employment section of the *Boston Globe,* I'd apply. Barring that, I wasn't sure where to begin other than continue to be on the alert for some inner guidance about what to do next.

About a month later, a friend who had been sick for a long time died. As I walked into the room for his funeral service I felt a strong inclination to sit next to a woman I hadn't met before. I briefly questioned why I should sit there when the room was full of people I knew. But the feeling was strong, and so I sat.

At the end of the service the woman and I exchanged pleasantries and she asked me what I did for a living. I don't know if you've ever had a time when your brain didn't engage with your mouth. This was one of those times for me. Despite the fact that my current job was as an operations manager, I answered, "I'm a psychic." I was immediately stricken with alarm. "Why did I answer this way?" "What will she think?!" I felt flustered by my answer. To my surprise (and relief) she was quite open and receptive.

She asked if she could book a session with me. Up until this time I had done readings only for friends and friends of friends.

This was a huge next step and I was very nervous. But again I found myself saying, "Of course," while my mind was saying, "No way!" I didn't have an office at that point, so we agreed to meet at her house the following week.

~~~

BILLFOLD BLESSING:
Bless this billfold, Lord, I pray.
Replenish it from day to day.
May the bills flow in and out,
Blessing people all about;
Help me earn and wisely spend;
Show me what to buy and lend.
Thank you, God, for bills to pay,
For the things I need today.
When 'tis empty, fill it more
From thy vast abundant store.
Amen.

ANONYMOUS

~~~

The session went great. She was thrilled. I was relieved. At the end of our time together, I asked, "What kind of work do you do?" She then told me that she was a writer for the *Boston Globe* and would love to write about her session in her column!

To make a long story short—she wrote the article, and in a very few months, more than four hundred people called to schedule appointments. Suddenly, I was running my own business! I believe my "Help Wanted" request to God and my willingness to follow my own inner guidance created a full-time business virtually overnight. I had a new office looking out onto a beautifully landscaped courtyard just as I had asked for.

Would you like to create your own "help wanted" ad? I don't have a lot of rules for this. I believe that God hears your desires even if you haven't expressed them as eloquently as you might have liked. You don't have to be a good writer or speller. You can use a computer or write the requests in pen, pencil, or crayon.

State your concerns. Dear God (Universe)—Here's what I'm worried about. Write a few paragraphs.

Say what you want and make it as specific as possible. Don't tell God *how* you want Him to answer you. He has amazing resources, well beyond our limited means, that can bring about miracles and fulfill our desires.

Allow for God's better idea! End with something that allows for the fact that God has a greater wisdom and may have better or different plans to resolve your issue. Conclude with something like, "God, if the above is in my highest interests, please work with me to bring this into my life. Thank you for all your blessings. I remain open to your guidance and direction."

Create a "mailbox" for your requests. I've had students who designed elaborate containers for their letters to God. They were beautifully painted works of art with inspiring words and symbols on them. Others have simply used a shoe box or Tupperware container, or created a special journal for the requests. God doesn't care what His mailbox looks like, but if it feels good to you to decorate it, please do!

Await a response. The answers come in varied ways depending on the nature of your request. You might want to keep notes of indications that your request is being answered. Pay attention to any flashes of insight, coincidences, synchronicities, a persistent thought that nudges you in a new direction, or any flickers of enthusiasm to contact someone or to start on a specific plan of action. God will begin putting the right people, ideas, and situations in your path so that your request will unfold in just the right way at just the right time and be a "win-win" solution for all involved.

Bob Scheinfeld, author of the book *The 11th Element,* uses a technique similar to the one I've described here. He adds another step, which I've just begun to implement myself. He periodically reviews his requests and finds they fall into four categories: (1) Still waiting for manifestation; (2) Need to revise; (3) Don't want anymore; and (4) Already fulfilled (or being fulfilled now). He calls this last one his "Got it!" file and returns to it often to enjoy all his successes.

Here is another example of a request I've made and the way it ultimately manifested with an invisible hand from my "Help Wanted" appeals.

Request:

I want a wonderful publisher for my next book. (In my actual request I described in more detail what "wonderful" meant.)

Universe responds: *Several publishers have my proposal for Compass of the Soul, and the decision-making process is maddeningly slow. During this time I receive an invitation to speak at a Unity Church in Kansas City, Missouri. Several days before my trip I realize that one of the publishers considering my proposal, Andrews McMeel, is headquartered there. Kansas City is a big place. I look on a map of the city and discover that my hotel is just two blocks away from them. I have an afternoon free so I call the editor who has my proposal and she agrees to see me. Several weeks later I have a signed contract from a publisher that perfectly matches the description of what I asked for in my request.*

What do *you* want help with? You have an amazing wealth of wisdom, intelligence, and connection that is available to you for the asking. Remember, don't try to figure out *how* you'll get something—just ask!

CHAPTER 9

The Prosperity Prayer

*Prayer programs divine guidance into the mental com-
puter. It is not an abdication of personal responsibility
but rather a profound taking of responsibility, the ultimate step toward our full divine empowerment on earth.*

MARIANNE WILLIAMSON

FOLLOWING IS THE PROSPERITY PRAYER THAT I WROTE SEVERAL
years ago. It's been circulating through the Internet for three-
plus years and I've received countless notes and letters from all
over the globe about its efficacy. When you say it, there's an
instant payoff—you feel better right away!

The Prosperity Prayer

Dear God—

I surrender my financial affairs and concerns about money to
your Divine care and love.

I ask that you remove my worries, anxieties, and fears about
money and replace them with faith.

I know and trust that my debts will be paid and money will flow into my life.

I have only to look to nature to see proof of the abundance you provide.

I release all negative thoughts about money and know that prosperity is my true state.

I commit to being grateful for all that I now have in my life.

I learn to manage my finances wisely, seeking help where needed.

And finally, I ask you to help me understand my purpose in life and to act on that purpose with courage and strength. I know that prosperity will come, in part, by doing work I love. Please help me use my skills and knowledge to be of service in the world.

Thank you, God.

Amen.

There is a great deal of research to indicate that if you want to create a new paradigm in your life, repeat that "new thing" every day for thirty days. My suggestion for working with the Prosperity Prayer is that you say it at least once a day for a month. Say it quietly to yourself or out loud. Write it down on a slip of paper so you can read it when you begin to feel old worries about money arise.

Following is a more detailed explanation about the philosophy behind the prayer.

Dear God—

God is a loaded word for many people. I believe that God is part of us, flows through us, and animates the world surrounding us.

We are programmed to receive God's wisdom. I see God as Divine Intelligence, Wisdom, and Love. Some people substitute the word *God* and use "Universe," "Lord," "Higher Self," or "Mother Father God." It doesn't matter what word you use for this prayer to work. Do you even have to believe in God? Not really. Simply know that your words are heard and expect an answer.

I surrender my financial affairs and concerns about money to your Divine care and love.

When we surrender our worries and concerns to God, we surrender to a Higher Power that has our best interests at heart. Surrender is a difficult concept for many of us to grasp. At first, it sounds as if I might be suggesting you simply "give up" in defeat or "let go" and pretend that your financial concerns do not matter.

Neither is true. The Wisdom that controls the universe knows how to make the sun rise in the morning and set at night. This Wisdom has created the human body and all its intricacies that function day in and day out in miraculous ways. It has created the eyes that read this page, the ears that hear the sounds around you, the sensation of touch as fingers turn this page.

Author and minister Marianne Williamson suggests that surrender is when "We learn to trust that the power that holds galaxies together can handle the circumstance of our relatively little lives." The Universe knows what it's doing! Can you say the same about your struggles with your financial life? If the issue of surrender is one that causes you a great deal of concern, I'd like to suggest an experiment—simply try it for a month. Read the Prosperity Prayer three times a day for thirty days and choose to "surrender your concerns" to God for that period of time. There is no right or wrong way to do this. The prayers of your heart will always be heard.

I ask that you remove my worries, anxieties, and fears about money and replace them with faith.

Many of us labor under the illusion that if we worry enough about money, we'll ward off debt. Nothing could be farther from the truth. Worry, anxiety, and fear create more worry, anxiety, and fear. They don't create more money. Again, for a thirty-day period I'd like to suggest you go on a worry diet. Become aware when you have fear-based and anxious thoughts. Remember the prayer and stop the worry process.

To live a truly prosperous life, you need to choose to let go of fear. It *is* a choice. Until you experience peace around the subject of money you will never be truly prosperous no matter how much money you have.

Here are some antiworry techniques that work:

If you find you simply can't ditch the worry habit, try limiting your worry to a five-minute period during a specific time of the day.

Find a phrase that you find comforting, such as "God is handling this now." Or "I choose to have faith about money." Or "I am now open and receptive to new avenues of income." Say it often.

Take action where necessary. Asking God to release your fears and replace them with faith does not absolve you from taking steps to untangle a difficult financial situation. What do you feel guided to do? Act on it.

Listen for guidance. Prayer is talking to God. Meditating and listening within are the ways you receive answers. Ask for help from God for ways you can begin to let go of fear and begin to prosper.

Confront your fear. Norman Vincent Peale wrote, "When you are afraid, do the thing you are afraid of and soon you will lose your fear of it." What's the worst thing that can happen to you regarding your concerns about money? What can you do to prevent worry from becoming reality? Do it.

Difficult times have helped me to understand better than before, how infinitely rich and beautiful life is in every way, and that so many things that one goes worrying about are of no importance whatsoever.

ISAK DINESEN

I know and trust that my debts will be paid and money will flow into my life.

Here's a secret I've discovered in working with my thousands of clients: there is tremendous power in the images you hold in your mind. These images (and the emotions they produce) begin to create the reality we experience in our lives. When you think about the topic of money, what pictures pop into your mind? Your maxed-out credit cards? Being a bag lady on the street? Not being able to pay the rent or mortgage? Continuing to struggle in a job you hate? Maybe you imagine the prospect of being poor the rest of your life?

If any of the above sound familiar, I'd like you to resolve to change these pictures in your mind. I'm asking you to accept much of this prayer philosophy on faith, but trust me when I tell you that the visualizations of your current state of poverty have a negative effect on your financial and emotional health.

Close your eyes for a moment and bring to mind an image of what it would look and feel like to have the prosperity you desire. Spend a few moments visualizing this perfect outcome. How would you feel if you got what you wanted? As you visualize this image, feel those emotions. Add some words to your imagery. Use whatever works for you. "This is great." "I feel terrific!" Imagine your friends and family celebrating with you. Do whatever you can to make this image real and vivid.

Ask God, "Is there anything I could do right now that would allow this prosperity to flow into my life?" Await a response.

Open your eyes when you feel ready. Jot down any brief ideas, thoughts, and impressions you may have had.

Don't take action simply on what you think makes sense. Act only on impulses that feel like fun, make you excited, or seem enjoyable to you. As you begin to change these images in your mind, the Universe will bring together the circumstances and synchronicities to enable you to have the prosperity you deserve. That's the trust part! Don't try to figure it out. Simply allow it to happen.

I have only to look to nature to see proof of the abundance you provide.

Abundance is our natural state. We disallow this state through our fear and worry. We cut ourselves off from its flow. The Bible says in Luke 12:32, "It is God's good pleasure to give you the kingdom." You may not be currently experiencing abundance in your wallet or checkbook but I assure you, it is there for the asking.

When you begin to worry that there isn't enough to go around or that God only doles out a limited supply of material to a deserving few, look around you. Take a deep breath and let in all of the abundance. Breathe the air (no limitations on that, right?). Look at your immediate environment. What do you see? Depending on the season and where you live, you'll see leaves on the trees, snow on the ground, sand on the beach, or grass on the lawns. Do you think God planned this amazing world and forgot to include the means for you to accomplish your purpose in life and live your dreams?

Each day as you say your Prosperity Prayer, spend a few moments to really take in the beauty and plenty in our world.

I release all negative thoughts about money and know that prosperity is my true state.

Your inner thoughts—what you say to yourself—make a big difference in your ability or inability to attract material wealth. When you consistently focus on negative thoughts you can count on attracting negativity into your life.

The next time a severe attack of "poverty consciousness" befalls you, counter it as lovingly as possible. Take a few minutes to sit quietly. Take a deep breath and imagine you are filled with and surrounded by God's love. Bring to mind the financial concern that is upsetting you and ask simply, "Is there another way of viewing this situation that will make me feel better?" Open your heart and your mind and await the answer. Often the mere fact that you've asked the question will bring about the shift in consciousness that you need. If you're faced with a difficult financial situation, affirm your ability to handle whatever comes your way and turn the problem over to God.

You might want to keep a stack of inspirational books, cards, audiotapes, or affirmations close at hand in order to help shift your focus. These are especially helpful for those of you who wake up in the middle of the night worrying about money. All the positive intentions in the world seem to fly out the window in those vulnerable hours before dawn.

I commit to being grateful for all that I now have in my life.

There are two quotes that I absolutely love that relate to the issue of gratitude. The first is from Meister Eckhart: "If the only prayer you say in your life is 'Thank you,' that would suffice." The second quote is from the famous writer Anonymous, who said, "If you want to feel rich, just count all of the things you have that money can't buy."

What is in your life right now that you feel grateful for? The word *abundance* does not just mean "financial prosperity." You are probably rich beyond measure in many areas of your life. Perhaps you are:

Rich in friends.

Overflowing with goodwill about your family.

Blessed with fantastic health.

Wealthy in positive life experience.

Affluent in knowledge and skill.

Prosperous with the nature surrounding your home.

When you begin to focus on appreciation, your intuition will constantly provide you with information about how to attain financial abundance. It will give you nudges, hints, impulses, feelings, hunches, and dreams to move you in the right direction. But in order to receive this Divine input, you must have a channel that's open to accepting its messages.

Sometimes the most important thing in a whole day is the rest we take between two deep breaths, or the turning inwards in prayer for five short minutes.

ETTY HILLESUM

I learn to manage my finances wisely, seeking help where needed.

It's been said that "God helps those who help themselves." This is especially true in the area of finances. In my work with clients, I've seen a clear correlation between how well they manage their money and their ability to attract more. Here's my advice—begin to learn about balancing your checkbook, debt consolidation (if appropriate), investment options, stocks, mutual funds, financial planners, and the like.

It might seem like a ridiculous assignment when you have negative dollars in your bank account or massive credit card debt, but do it anyway. There are three main reasons for this:

1. You begin to attract what you focus on. By looking at ways to manage your money, you are focusing your attention on prosperity, not the lack of it.

2. You will need to have this knowledge in order to wisely invest the money you bring in through the Prosperity Prayer. Remember that annoying adage, "The rich get richer, the poor get poorer"? Part of the reason for this is that the wealthy know how to manage their money well. Acting as if you are wealthy is a powerful tool for attracting what you desire.

3. Learning about money management can be a bit overwhelming at first. You don't need to be an expert. Start with small things such as reading a beginner's book on finances. Or pick up any one of the monthly money magazines that attract you and seem easy to understand. If you're online, there are many helpful sites to visit. The learning curve may feel a bit steep, so at first just read the material to get familiar with the terminology. Don't skip this step because it "isn't spiritual." We live in a material and practical world and it helps to know the rules of the road.

And finally, I ask you to help me understand my purpose in life and to act on that purpose with courage and strength. I know that prosperity will come, in part, by doing work I love. Please help me use my skills and knowledge to be of service in the world.

You have a purpose in life. It is the thing about which you are excited, the thing you'd love to do if only you had a few million dollars and didn't have to worry about money. Do it anyway! When you are enthusiastic about something in your life, God is giving you a clue about the direction to follow. The root of the word "enthusiasm" is from the Greek *entheos*. It literally means "God within."

Begin to trust the passion that you feel. When you listen to the whispers of your soul and take small steps forward, your life purpose begins to take shape and manifest clearly. It takes courage, trust, and strength to begin to live the life you were meant to live. You have access to the gift of divine guidance to help you begin to fulfill your destiny. Each time you pray for help and you act on the guidance you receive, you align your mind with the mind of God. You tap into a stream of love and intelligence that will direct you to the prosperity that will help you fulfill your destiny.

Thank you, God.
I know you are there to help me and I am grateful.
Amen.

Prayer is your divine connection to God. It allows you to enter the sphere of love, support, abundance, and wisdom that is your birthright. When you pray, you allow the energy of All-That-Is to flow through you and create miracles in your life. If you haven't been a "praying person" give it a try. It can't hurt and I promise . . . it can only help.

CHAPTER 10

How Much Is Enough?

We must become artists in living. To live by inspiration means to sense the divine touch in everything; to enter into the spirit of things; to enter into the joy of living.

ERNEST HOLMES

THE DEFINITION OF PROSPERITY IN ITS BROADEST SENSE IS "SPIRI-tual well-being." It is not just about having sufficient money in the bank or in your pocketbook. You have only to glance at the headlines in a magazine or newspaper to see examples of wealthy people who are unhappy. Hugh Downs, the news commentator, said it well: "A happy person is not a person in a certain set of circumstances but rather a person with a certain set of attitudes." Prosperity is about knowing that you have the tools and resources to live a healthy, exciting, and joy-filled life.

Joey Dugan was a client I worked with for several years. He was a charming and charismatic man with an easy laugh. Money seemed to flow into his life at every turn. He had been riding high for many years through the construction and sale of new homes and office complexes. He said he had felt omnipotent. The risks were exciting and he enjoyed creating a larger and larger real estate empire.

One day I arrived at his office for our consulting session. He looked uncharacteristically despondent and confessed that despite all the money he was making, he felt empty. The acquisition of money, power, and fame had motivated him for a long time. Now that he had all that he ever wanted and more, he didn't know what to do. He said, "It's like I've run off the edge of the map and I don't know which way to head next."

I suggested that instead of creating business strategies as we had planned, we should talk about what made him happy. It was time for the creation of new goals. I asked, "If all of your wealth was taken away tomorrow, where would you begin again?"

While it may seem surprising to you that someone with "all that money" could be distressed, it happens to many of us—rich or poor—if we don't stay tuned in to our life purpose, hopes, and dreams. Money doesn't solve problems of the soul. In some ways it may even complicate them. Many people with a great deal of material wealth find themselves stuck in the rut of believing that simply acquiring more "stuff" will make them happy. That path may provide short-term relief as they enjoy their latest toy but it's doomed as a vehicle for long-term change and happiness.

Here is another simple truth—no matter how much money a person has, he or she usually wants more. Think of this in your own life. When you were starting out and making a small amount of money, you probably thought that a 10 percent raise would bring within reach a good many things that you wanted. That relatively small raise might have given you a vacation, a better car, or nicer clothes.

Fast-forward a few years and perhaps you're making 30 percent more than in your entry-level position. You're able to take a vacation every year, have a nice car, and wear fashionable clothes. What do you want now? Perhaps you could buy your first home or take a more expensive vacation.

Move ahead several more years, and with an increase in salary your dreams have expanded even more. Now you want a bigger home for your growing family or a larger car, or perhaps it's time to think of private schools for the children.

I recently spoke with a woman who has a multimillion-dollar trust fund. She has enough money for most families to live in great ease for the rest of their lives. However, she still felt limited by her income. In her social group of neighbors and friends, it was very important to wear the right kind of jewelry and clothes in order to be accepted and fit in. She had just bought a $25,000 necklace and was concerned that in order to feel comfortable in her role in society she needed to buy several more pieces of equal or greater value.

That's all pretty depressing and will probably leave many of you asking, "How much is enough?" If what I've said is true, prosperity will always feel as near as the next raise, lottery win, or insurance settlement. In other words, prosperity is right around the next corner. But that's not a great way to live, is it? It's the kind of thinking that allows you to max out your credit cards, gamble frequently, and live on the edge financially because you'll get that big payoff "someday soon."

So, what's the solution to this age-old dilemma? The answer lies in a seeming contradiction—

What you have in your life right now is enough.

It's okay to want more.

When I say, "You have enough," it may seem laughable. You can look around your poorly furnished house, at your desk with unpaid bills, your empty refrigerator, and your car that breaks down every week and see great evidence to the contrary.

But I'm talking about "enough" as a state of consciousness. If you can master the following way of thinking about prosperity, you will change the way money flows to you. The tide of abundance will become more plentiful and life will become peaceful. Here is an example of the way a prosperous person thinks:

"I choose to focus on all that I have right now, rather than on lack and struggle. I feel at peace and know that all my needs are met. Ideas and opportunities to improve my financial situation present themselves at just the right time. I act on these with ease and enthusiasm. I always have enough for what I truly need and want."

Let go of your struggle with money; abundance is your natural state of being. If you can't quite imagine this to be true for you, try it out as an idea for the next few months, experiment with the thought, or play it out in your mind. Ask yourself, "What would a person who truly feels prosperous be thinking right now?"

Most people believe that when they have lots of money, they will feel prosperous. I maintain it is the other way around. When you . . .

Feel prosperous

See abundance all around you

Know that you are safe

Understand that you are worthy just as you are

Imagine a joy-filled life

Let go of struggle . . .

You will experience the state of *Divine Prosperity*. It's a state of mind and spirit that brings about the life you love and the abundance you deserve.

It is not always easy to move from a place of worrying about your lack of money all the time to feeling at peace about money. Taking small "abundance breaks" throughout the day is a great way to begin.

When we seek money, or a good relationship, or
a great job, what we are really seeking is happiness.
The mistake we make is not going for happiness first.
If we did, everything else would follow.

DEEPAK CHOPRA

When you start to feel anxious about the topic of money—catch yourself—stop.

Take a slow, deep breath.

Connect with God in whatever way feels appropriate and ask for help in shifting your thoughts.

Continue to do this for a few moments and begin to focus on anything at all that makes you feel better. This might be your daughter's smile, a cat's purr, the sun on your skin, or the scent of the flowers outside your door. It doesn't matter what it is, as long as you shift your thoughts.

Take one final, slow, deep breath. As you inhale say to yourself, "I am at peace. Abundance surrounds and fills my life. All is well."

Exhale and return to this exercise as often as needed.

Now, take out your prosperity journal and ask yourself what the following means to you: "What you have in your life right now is enough." Write down your thoughts about this, then write about some of the ways you've kept prosperity from flowing freely in your life. Finally, write about what you will do to change. Your answers will give you some useful insight into what—and how—you think about money.

You may find yourself among the many who believe more money equals more happiness. If so, I have some news you'll probably find fascinating. Richard Easterlin, an economist with the University of Southern California, surveyed fifteen hundred people on this topic over a period of three decades, and his findings reveal that the true source of happiness for most of us is more time with family and friends, plus—you guessed it—good health.

University of Illinois psychologist Ed Diener backs up Easterlin's findings. He surveyed the Forbes 100 wealthiest Americans and discovered they're only slightly happier than the rest of us. Diener's research confirms that those whose incomes have increased over a ten-year period are not happier than those whose income has not increased.

Dr. David G. Meyers, an authority on the psychology of happiness, says we should understand "that enduring happiness doesn't come from success. People adapt to changing circumstances—even to wealth or a disability. Thus wealth is like health: its utter absence breeds misery, but having it (or any circumstance we long for) doesn't guarantee happiness."

The University of Chicago's National Opinion Research Center (CNORC) has been surveying people in the United States on the topic of happiness since 1957. Since that time, the number of people indicating they are "very happy" has declined from 35 percent to 30 percent. And during that time, Americans have become twice as rich and a little less happy. In fact, between 1956 and 1988, the percentage of Americans who said they were satisfied with their financial situation dropped from 42 percent to 30 percent.

So, what *does* make people happy? According to the CNORC surveys, people with five or more close friends are 50 percent more likely to describe themselves as "very happy" than respondents with fewer close friends. Forty percent of people who reported being "very happy" were in a loving marriage. And lastly, good health and a connection to community or a religious group seemed to round out the happiness indicators.

The lesson? Continue to be open to abundance. But keep your focus on the qualities that will make you truly happy. Love, forgiveness, kindness, charity, and service are the real attributes of a life well lived.

CHAPTER 11

Prosperity Is Seeking You

Billfold Blessing: Bless this billfold, Lord, I pray. Replenish it from day to day. May the bills flow in and out, blessing people all about. Help me earn and wisely spend. Show me what to buy and lend. Thank you, God, for bills to pay, for the things I need today. When 'tis empty, fill it more, from thy vast abundant store. Amen.

ANONYMOUS

I'M STARTING THIS CHAPTER WITH AN EASY POP QUIZ. WHICH OF THE following two people would you guess was the more prosperous?

Person #1: "I hesitate to try anything new because a problem might arise and just cause more trouble in my life. I don't like change. It's hard for me to trust others because they might take advantage of any new ideas I have. I feel resentful of people who have more money than me. Life isn't fair. I don't know why things seem to work out for everyone else but they don't for me. I guess I was just born unlucky."

Person #2: "I take appropriate risks. I feel confident in my ability to create new and wonderful things in my life. People generally like and trust me and I like and trust others. I know that I build my self-esteem each time I take a small or large step toward my goals and I succeed. I appreciate life and all that I have."

I know that the answer is pretty obvious. You immediately want to vote for Person #2. You have a feeling that you could probably trust him to manage your investments or to handle a special project at work. You might even like to have him over for dinner to discuss business opportunities. This man draws money to him because he feels worthy of it and he respects himself enough to be cautious with it.

You have to count on living every single day
in a way you believe will make you feel good
about your life—so that if it were over tomorrow,
you'd be content with yourself.

JANE SEYMOUR

When I listen to people who are successful, happy, and prosperous I hear a consistent theme. They envision success and have a positive expectation of success, and their thoughts and actions are consistent with the anticipation of prosperity and abundance. They play out their dreams and ambitions in their minds, listen to their inner guidance, and take action on its wisdom. You might think of them as merely *lucky*. I see it differently. It's as if prosperity and success seek them out. They magnetize what they want to create through the power of their mind and emotion.

If you can stretch your imagination a bit further, consider that there is an "abundance energy" that permeates the very air around us. Do you think our Person #1 is going to be very attractive to this abundance? My guess is that even if he did manage to draw some money his way, it would soon disappear. Conversely, if our Person #2 begins to attract abundance, you have no doubt that he will respect it, treat it wisely, and invest it well.

What about you? When you think about the topic of prosperity and living a rich life what do your thoughts dwell on? Try the following exercise and see.

1. When I think about the topic of money, I feel hopeful and optimistic.
- ☐ Most of the time
- ☐ Sometimes
- ☐ Rarely

2. I feel proud of my accomplishments.
- ☐ Most of the time
- ☐ Sometimes
- ☐ Rarely

3. I feel confident that I create what I want in life.
- ☐ Most of the time
- ☐ Sometimes
- ☐ Rarely

4. I take time for fun, enjoyable, creative activities.
- ☐ Most of the time
- ☐ Sometimes
- ☐ Rarely

5. I make time for spiritual and personal development.

☐ Most of the time

☐ Sometimes

☐ Rarely

6. People seem to like and trust me.

☐ Most of the time

☐ Sometimes

☐ Rarely

7. I manage my finances wisely. Each month I balance my checkbook and stay aware of the status of all my investments.

☐ Most of the time

☐ Sometimes

☐ Rarely

8. I feel that I'm a good person who is worthy of having an abundance of money.

☐ Most of the time

☐ Sometimes

☐ Rarely

9. I take time each day to appreciate all that I have.

☐ Most of the time

☐ Sometimes

☐ Rarely

10. I take small steps and appropriate risks so that I feel excited and enthusiastic about my life.

☐ Most of the time

☐ Sometimes

☐ Rarely

11. I stay away from situations that continually drain my energy or I resolve them.

☐ Most of the time
☐ Sometimes
☐ Rarely

12. I love to learn new things and make time to read, take classes, or otherwise educate myself.

☐ Most of the time
☐ Sometimes
☐ Rarely

13. I frequently check in with my "inner prosperity guide"— my intuition—to direct me on the path to success.

☐ Most of the time
☐ Sometimes
☐ Rarely

If you circled an abundance of "most of the time" answers:

You feel good about yourself and take time for fun and personal self-care. You've made a lot of progress in the self-esteem department. Your intuition communicates with you in so many ways. Your job is to keep the lines of transmission open and check in with your inner guidance whenever you have a doubt, question, or concern. The answers are always there, directing you to the prosperity you deserve. As you ask for direction, the answers begin to flow. You stand at all times in a Universe full of abundance and love. As you continue to embrace it, your life will begin to unfold in miraculous ways.

If you circled mostly "sometimes" answers:

Don't stop when things are just satisfactory; continue to take small steps toward your ultimate happiness, even when that route takes you out of your comfort zone. When you follow your intuition it will invariably lead you to a life of joy. Your intuition is a guide to your prosperity. When you trust its wisdom and take action on the information you receive, doors open, opportunities appear, synchronicities occur. Don't try to logically figure out how you'll achieve your goals. There's an element of trust in this process. Johann Wolfgang von Goethe said, "Whatever you can do, or dream you can, begin it. Boldness has genius, power, and magic in it." Intention has power and miracles do happen! How would someone act who had achieved your goal? Act as if success is certain. Know that you'll create your dreams.

The future belongs to those who dare.

ANONYMOUS

If you circled mostly "rarely" answers:
Expect a few setbacks on the road to prosperity. They're a natural part of the process in creating a life you love, and we've all managed to get through them. They help us to grow and learn. Don't view them or yourself as a failure because you ran into an obstacle. Pick yourself up, continue to experiment, and proceed with all the fearlessness you can muster. Ask yourself what you learned and get back on your path. *Want* your goal enthusiastically. Shift your focus from "I can't" to "How can I?" Talk to people who will be supportive of you and your goal. Take some small steps toward your dream and keep walking! You'll get there!

CHAPTER 12

The Path to a Debt-Free Life

I had plastic surgery last week. I cut up my credit cards.

HENNY YOUNGMAN

JANE SAT IN MY OFFICE WITH TEARS STREAMING DOWN HER FACE. "This creating abundance idea just doesn't seem to work for me. I work hard and hold down two jobs and I still can't pay the bills. I'm sick and tired of being sick and tired. I think I'll be poor the rest of my life."

There are probably few of us who haven't felt that way at one time or another. You might have arrived there after you were laid off from a job, or unexpectedly saddled with a huge medical bill or after a divorce. Whatever the circumstances, it doesn't feel good. You try and you try and nothing seems to change. You feel stuck in an endless cycle of working more and saving less. Your whole being is focused on the bills, the debt, and the hopelessness of it all.

Jane isn't alone. The average American family has credit card debt of $8,400 and about 20 percent have "maxed out" their credit cards. The Federal Reserve reports that over 40 percent of American families spend more than they earn. If you're in this situation, what can you do to prevent falling into a state of poverty and despair? You have three main choices: (1) You can give up, yell, "I can't take it anymore!" and hope that someone or something comes along to rescue you. (This doesn't usually happen.) (2) You can just keep doing what you're doing. (Things will probably remain the same or get worse.) (3) You can choose a new destination, the one called "abundance," and put one foot ahead of the other and keep walking.

I'm guessing you want to land in abundance rather than farther in debt, so let's figure out the best path to get you there! Several of the steps below will immediately generate cash in hand to assist you in debt reduction. Other tips will help you attract the abundance you're looking for.

Hold your focus on prosperity—This may not be as easy as it seems at first. In all likelihood you've spent a lot of time thinking about how broke you are and wasted a lot of emotional energy on feeling afraid. This happens whenever you're dwelling on depressing thoughts about the mortgage that's due in a few days or the bill collector who called yesterday asking for a payment on your overdue credit card.

Remember—you attract what you habitually focus on. So what do you do to break the cycle? When those habitual thoughts come to mind, greet them gently, then focus on what you want instead. Some people find it helpful to have a word, action, or phrase to break the habit of poverty consciousness. A friend of mine simply thinks the word "Next!" when trying to shift her focus. Another person carries a small stone with the word "prosperity" engraved on it. She touches it often to remind her of her ultimate intention. What would work for you?

Speak positively about money—In other words, stop talking about how broke you are. It may be true that you're currently in a state of financial hardship. However, the surest way to stay there is to tell the world about how bad it is! Now you not only have your own energy focused on it but everyone else's as well!

Let your mind dance in a world beyond the obvious,
and you will access a cache of treasures more glorious
than those of the world's wealthiest billionaire.

ALAN COHEN

Which of these two sentiments feels better to you? "I'm poor. I'm broke. I don't have enough money. Things don't work out for me." Or, "Things are turning around. I have a plan of action. I know things are beginning to look up for me." It takes some discipline to catch yourself and shift your thoughts, feelings, and words, but it will make all the difference in creating the new, prosperous life circumstances you desire.

Release clutter and create cash—Feng shui experts tell us that letting go of what you don't want, clearing up clutter, and organizing what's left will help you create "flowing energy" that opens you up for more abundance in your life. Just as important, selling or trading or giving away these items to charity can be a source of income as well.

What do you have in your home or office that you don't use? Are there clothes you no longer wear or a record collection that's collecting dust? Take a look at everything you haven't used in over a year. Consider donating your things to a charity and getting a receipt for your taxes at the end of the year. Keep a record of your donations. Your gifts of clothing or household items can add up to a significant reduction in your taxes. To create some cash in hand, think about a yard sale, place a classified ad, or go on eBay to sell these items.

Pay attention to the small money—Your debt didn't just happen overnight. You can probably attribute it to the big-ticket items; the car you bought two years ago, the vacation you took last winter, or the new career wardrobe. What might surprise you, however, is how quickly the small items add up. My husband and I tried an experiment. We bought small notebooks and individually wrote down every item we paid cash for during a one-month period. At the end of thirty days we reviewed our lists filled with notations about muffins, bottled water, magazines, juice, coffee, occasional lunches and movies—nothing wrong with that. But we were shocked by how much it added up to!

If you're like many people, you might grab a sandwich for lunch at the local deli. Let's say that a combination of a soft drink, chips, and sandwich cost on average around $7.00. If you have lunch out every day, that is $35 a week. If you multiply that by fifty-two weeks a year, that adds up to $1,820 a year. That would be a tidy sum to put into a retirement fund or to pay down your debt. It's enough to make PBJ sandwiches for lunch every day sound perfectly reasonable! Understand that I'm not encouraging you to give up on deli lunches, magazines, your morning coffee, or anything else that is fun for you. I'm suggesting that you consciously choose what you want to spend your money on. Try this experiment for a month and see where your money goes.

Create a financial abundance plan—There are few things worse than the sinking feeling you get when you open a bill and you don't know where the money will come from to pay it. You start with self-recrimination: "How did I let this happen?" and move on to hopelessness, "I'll never get ahead." You are instantly plunged into despair. Hold on before you beat yourself up further. It's just a piece of paper. It doesn't represent you, your self-worth, your intelligence, or your potential. The fact is, governments throughout the world survive on debt, so you have plenty of company.

Most of us feel incredibly ashamed when we have an out-of-control financial situation. There are many ways to deal with this state of affairs, from dysfunctional—throwing the bills away or avoiding the debt collectors—to functional—having a plan of action to pay down the debt. The latter not only will make you feel better, but it's also the only thing that will work in the long run. If the task of paying down your bills feels truly overwhelming to you, get help. A good financial planner or a reputable credit-counseling service may be a good place to begin. They'll not only negotiate lower monthly fees for many credit cards, but they'll also stick with you and come up with a plan to prioritize payments, helping you save money.

Most important, from a consciousness point of view, your energy will be freed up to begin attracting the money you deserve. Here's another way to think about this. Suppose you have a friend who is totally disorganized about money. She's constantly in debt and has no idea how much she has or how much she has available to spend each month. Would you want to lend her money? No. The message that she presents to you is, "I'm not good with money." That's the message she presents to the Universe as well. Given what you've read so far in this book, do you think she's someone who radiates the energy to attract abundance?

Appreciate your bills—I swear I haven't gone off the deep end on this one! But to be more specific, appreciate what your bills *represent*. You have a mortgage bill because you have a wonderful home to live in. You have a dentist bill because your teeth are healthy and pain-free. The student loan payment represents a college education that will help you earn more money in a job you love. The grocery receipts signify your ability to feed your family. See? It's all in the way you think about it!

Today I will plan my finances and accept what has to be, always trusting in the Universe to provide.

YVONNE KAYE

As you pay down your bills or pay them off completely, remember to thank the Universe for the prosperity you have. Gratitude attracts more abundance. Each time you sit down with your checkbook, send off a silent prayer of thanks. Thanks for the money that you have, the money that will continue to come in the future, and for all that you presently have in your life that money has purchased in the past. Open your heart to the channel of abundance and proclaim, "Money flows into my life. I am open and receptive to all avenues of income."

CHAPTER 13

Success Steps on the Road to Wealth

We're looking for that chemistry that's so strong it sparks our passion. That kind of clarity, I've learned, is very rare. Most people just take one step at a time. They follow an inkling, and they grow into or stumble onto—something they love, discovering talents they didn't know they had.

PO BRONSON

I RECENTLY HAD LUNCH WITH A COLLEAGUE. THIS WAS THE FIRST time Janet and I had gotten together outside of the professional organization we belonged to. We gave each other a brief history of our individual career twists and turns. Janet had been laid off from a job as an estate lawyer years ago and had turned her passion for educating people about money management into a new career as a speaker, consultant, and writer. I spoke about the time I had moved to New York to take a job with a start-up company only to have it fold after I'd been there two months. Shortly after that I began to take the first steps on the path to what became my life career.

It occurred to me during our conversation that the times in both our lives when things seemed the most bleak were, in fact, launching pads for new careers, opportunities, life fulfillment, and increased prosperity. It just didn't seem so at the time. I remember all too clearly the fear, worry, and anxiety that consumed me after I lost my job. Yet, here I am many years later looking back at those events and recognizing the Divine hand that played a role in all that unfolded. During the time it was happening I was too close to see it. How much better I would have felt if I knew then what I know now. What looked like a dead end or at least a detour was really a series of success steps that got me going in the right direction.

Very few people are overnight successes. "I don't know how to do it! I don't know how to get from here to there!" is the protest I hear from many people when we discuss living a life of their dreams. Not being able to figure out exactly how to get from the desire phase to the achievement stage perplexes all of us. It's the part that requires faith, trust, courage, and inner guidance. However, all successful people were beginners once. They started out just like you and me, most not quite sure how to find the path to the goals they wanted to achieve. They learned to take small steps to get where they wanted to go.

When you learn to listen to your inner prosperity guide—your intuition—*you'll* be given a step-by-step road map to your goals. What could you do today? Is there anything that's right in front of you that holds some interest or passion? Your inner guidance may give you a nudge toward something that might not make logical sense. However, it's important to learn to trust those impulses. They will almost always lead you back to the path heading in the right direction. Your rational mind will help you figure out where you want to go. Your intuitive mind will show you the most direct path.

All of us at one time or another have had to make a major life change. It may have been because you were fired or laid off or because you had to move to another state with your company. The change may have been the result of a health crisis that prevented you from working for a period of time. Sometimes the change is not something thrust on you but something you have chosen. You may have decided to go back to school, change careers, or to stay home with a child.

Heighten your ability to stay in the flow by heading out, talking to people, making contacts, stepping out from where it's safe and cozy, pushing against your comfort zones, and reaching out. That's how the faucet of flow is turned on—by generating energy each day so the Universe-at-Large can engage its magnificent laws and deliver to you even more energy.

STUART WILDE

How do you know when it's the right time to make a change and begin to take the small steps that will hopefully lead you to success and greater abundance? Here are some points to ponder that may help you decide:

Are you bored with what you do? Boredom is one of those messages from your intuition that change is needed. It's a signal that your energy is being drained and that something new needs to happen. Bear in mind that the change that's required may simply be a shift in attitude or a new way of approaching something. It could also mean it is time to take action and make an outer, tangible change in your life.

How will you feel if you don't make the change? This is a powerful question to ask. Imagine yourself a few months to a few years in the future. Envision your life if you *don't* make the change you're contemplating. If the predominant feeling is one of regret and sadness it's time to make the leap and do the thing you want to do. Are you guaranteed smooth sailing from here on in? No. I read a quote recently by Marilyn Moats Kennedy. She said, "It's better to be boldly decisive and risk being wrong than to agonize at length and be right too late."

What are five "action steps" you could take? Look at your list and ask yourself which one has the most vitality. Is there one that stands out that makes you feel excited and passionate? These strong feelings are another intuitive indicator that you're heading in the right direction. Remember, this doesn't need to be a huge leap. If it feels too big, there are probably some ways that you could break it down into smaller, less risky steps.

What's the worst that could happen? It's normal to feel at least a little anxious when you're about to do something new and different. This is the time to use the left side of your brain—the logical side—to reflect on the possible consequences of your actions. Just don't belabor this part! Be both realistic and creative. Do you have enough money to support you during a transition? If not, what are some innovative ways to create financial reserves? Whom will your decision impact? Make sure they're on board. What do you need in order to make the change as easy and effortless as possible?

⁓

The secret of getting ahead is getting started.
The secret of getting started is breaking your complex,
overwhelming tasks into small manageable tasks,
and then starting on the first one.

MARK TWAIN

⁓

In her *O* magazine, Oprah Winfrey stated, "I believe we discover our destinies in the smallest ways—in a fascination with words, in the thrill a child's laughter evokes, and even in a familiar song we keep humming. If you pay attention to the cues—to the time you've felt most joyous, most fully engaged, most connected with yourself and others—you'll always be guided to the next best place." Where do you feel guided to begin? What needs to be done first? Where can you make a difference today?

What are some things that call to you? If you haven't done so, write down what you really want and be as specific as possible. Write down everything you know about your desired work. Describe an ideal day, week, month, year. How much money would you like to have or earn? What kind of a home would you like to have? Describe the kind of car you'd like to drive. Put anything on this list that is important to your ideal life and keep it in a place where you'll see it every day.

Use visual motivators. I have a collage on the wall in front of my desk that visually illustrates what I want to create. You might have a lucky charm that you carry with you or a poem that inspires you. Your visual cue might be a photo of you taken at a moment when you looked and felt great. If you feel inspired when you see these objects then what you have chosen is perfect.

Listen to and read inspiring words. Buy or rent audiotapes or CDs of motivational speakers. Listen to these as you're going to work in the morning or before you go to bed at night. There is research that indicates *hearing* something imprints the message differently in the brain over *reading* something. If it works, why not do both? If you feel the need for encouragement to get you out of a poverty rut and into a prosperity stream, read books about people who have taken their own success steps and created a life they love.

The philosopher Epictetus shared his version of the wisdom of taking small steps when he said, "Nothing great is created suddenly, any more than a bunch of grapes or a fig. If you tell me that you desire a fig, I answer you that there must be time. Let it first blossom, than bear fruit, then ripen." Be gentle with yourself as you create change in your life. Let yourself be open to the unfolding process and follow your inner wisdom. It will always lead you in the right direction.

CHAPTER 14

Gratitude = Financial Miracle-Gro

It's good to have money and the things that money can buy, but it's good, too, to check up once in a while and make sure you haven't lost the things money can't buy.

GEORGE LORIMER

I'M SURE YOU'VE SEEN SOMETHING LIKE THE FOLLOWING IN A NEWS-paper or financial magazine. "Dear Financial Adviser: I am twenty-seven years old and my wife is twenty-five. We have two young children. We have $350,000 equity in our house, $450,000 in X Mutual Fund, and $225,000 in Y Mutual Fund. Our annual income is $150,000...." I don't know about you, but I've usually tuned out by the third sentence.

If we're honest, most of us compare ourselves to others and wonder if we measure up. It's hard to miss the stories of folks who have "made it." The news media are full of information about the price of Madonna's gown, the latest high-priced gadget, or the cost of a fabulous piece of real estate purchased by a big-name celebrity. What usually happens is that you begin to think about all that you *don't have* and you feel poorer still by comparison.

I suggest you work at shifting the focus on those inner judgments and come home to what's real for you. Begin to express gratitude for what you already have. The truth is, what you focus on expands. Do you want to enlarge the feeling of scarcity and lack by the relentless comparisons? Or do you want to increase your abundance by focusing your appreciation on what you already have?

In moments when things look bleak—especially
in those moments—see only perfection, express
only gratefulness, and imagine only what
manifestation of perfection you choose next.

NEALE DONALD WALSCH

Just for a moment, bring to mind something that someone else has that you want. It could be a brand-new car, a designer outfit, a huge house, or an item of jewelry. Sit with the comparison for about thirty seconds. How do you feel? Words that I frequently hear from people doing this exercise are: constricted, empty, worthless, jealous, hopeless, resentful, and despairing. You know deep down in your soul that those are not feelings that enhance prosperity or financial well-being. It's almost as if those strong emotions set up a resistance energy that pushes away the good things that you desire.

Now try the opposite. Think of something you currently have in your life that you feel great about. You could choose to reflect on less material items such as the fact that you have good friends, kind neighbors, great health, a supportive spouse, or terrific kids. Sit with those thoughts of gratitude for the same thirty seconds and take note of how you feel at the end of that time. You will probably use words such as open, thankful, strong, happy, hopeful, refreshed, appreciative, and invigorated. What's your guess about which group of thoughts and feelings makes you more open to receiving more abundant blessings into your life?

Oprah Winfrey stated this concept well when she said, "When you dwell on all the reasons you have to be grateful, you open yourself to receiving even more good—and more good comes to you. As you begin to feel abundant, you'll be willing and able to pass positive things on to others."

Gratitude is truly the Miracle-Gro for an abundant and prosperous life. What do you want to grow? If you pour the fertilizer on thoughts like, "I don't have enough," "I'll never get out of debt," or "We'll never be able to afford that," you'll just be proliferating weeds. Conversely, think about what happens if you pour the fertilizer on prospering and grateful thoughts. "We have wonderful, healthy food to eat." "My car is running well and gets me to and from my job." "It's good to have a job in a down economy." "I appreciate my healthy body and the energy I have to do all the things I want." Those are the thoughts that grow a rich life and attract the material wealth you desire and deserve.

Get into the habit of observing and noting abundance wherever you see and experience it. You'll stay stuck in scarcity if you focus on what you don't have. It just takes practice to shift the focus from lack to abundance. Prosperity is not something *out there* waiting for us to find it. It is something that exists now. It is the natural state of the Universe. When you are grateful, you are not blocking the flow of abundance, you are opening to it.

A grateful and generous heart is like a magnet. When you take the time to acknowledge the abundance in your life and share the wealth, you attract even more blessings and reasons to feel grateful. In this way, receiving and giving creates a circle of energy that serves us all.

CHERYL RICHARDSON

What are you grateful for? Here are some ideas to get you started:

1. What do you like about your work?

2. How would you describe the three nicest qualities of your spouse?

3. What does your best friend do to support you that makes you glad he or she is your friend?

4. Describe something you're proud of achieving this week, month, or year.

5. What were your kids doing the last time they made you laugh?

6. What do you love about your home?

7. What makes you smile?

8. Describe something you currently own that you're especially proud of.

9. When you're out in nature, what makes your heart soar?

10. What positive quality did you develop as the result of your upbringing?

I'm not suggesting that you're required to jump for joy when something bad happens, but that you're simply open to a new way of viewing life from the present moment. Eckhart Tolle, author of *The Power of Now,* suggests that "When you are full of problems, there is no room for anything new to enter, no room for a solution. So whenever you can, make some room, create some space, so that you find the life underneath your life situation."

Find a way to shift the way you look at what is happening in your life and imbue it with gratitude. That's one of the ways to create the space that Tolle speaks of. Use all your senses. What are the sounds you hear? The scents you smell? What do you view around you? Observe the rhythm of life flowing in you and all around you. Be in the present moment and find the place in your heart and soul where you know you are okay. Focus on your breathing and connect with God in your thoughts. Know you are safe, loved, and protected and that all that the Universe has is yours.

Every night before you go to bed, think of three things that happened that day for which you feel grateful. I believe that if you will commit to this for one month, you will notice some very positive things.

- You'll feel happier and more joy-filled.

- People will like being around you.

- Your life will take on new meaning.

- Your relationship with others will improve.

- You'll start seeing possibilities rather than limitations.

- Intuitive information will flow to you more easily.

- You'll be "luckier." People and circumstances will begin to conspire in your favor.

- Prosperity-producing ideas and concepts will pop into your mind and you'll be able to act on their wisdom.

- Life in general and your life in particular will begin to feel more abundant and full of possibilities.

- Money will begin to find new avenues to flow into your life.

There is an old saying, "I had the blues because I had no shoes, until upon the street, I met a man who had no feet." How many times have you overlooked the plenty that is all around you and failed to appreciate it? When you begin to have an attitude of gratitude toward what you already have, you'll multiply the abundance in all areas of your life.

CHAPTER 15

The Life You Were Born to Live

Each soul comes to the Earth with gifts [and] enters into a sacred agreement with the Universe to accomplish specific goals.... Whatever the task your soul has agreed to, whatever its contract with the Universe, all of the experiences of your life serve to awaken within you the memory of that contract, and to prepare you to fulfill it.

GARY ZUKAV

AS A CHILD I WAS FASCINATED BY THE UNSEEN WORLD. I WOULD spend hours with the kids in the neighborhood playing a game I made up called Angels and Mortals. I have no idea how I came up with the name and only a sketchy memory of how the game was played. When I was a teenager, I studied religion, philosophy, psychology, and books on ESP and I loved to write. I believe there was something deep within me, even as a child, that directed me to the work I would ultimately do as an adult.

What about you? What were you passionately interested in as a child? Did you love to draw or take photographs, or have dreams of becoming an actress? Perhaps you were drawn to more scholarly pursuits and enjoyed researching favorite topics or studying how things worked. Whatever it was, know that there is a clue in your early beginnings that points you in the direction of your true soul work.

If you start work at age twenty, work forty hours a week and retire at age sixty-five, you will have worked almost one hundred thousand hours. Wouldn't it be wonderful to spend those hours doing something you're passionate about and something that allows you to contribute your unique skill and interest to the world? If you don't begin now, when will you do it? It's not something that needs to happen overnight. All that is required of you right now is that you make a commitment to begin the process of uncovering your life mission. You don't have to know what it is or even how you'll make a living at it right now. Take it one step at a time. This is a process that will unfold in stages.

Determine whether it's time for a change. How do you feel when you get up in the morning? Do you dread the day ahead of you? Are you tired, bored, and exhausted? Those are all clues from your inner guidance that it's time for a change. There may be other situations beyond your work that cause you to feel this way. However, work is often the culprit simply because of the number of waking hours we spend at our jobs. Here are some issues to think about:

1. Do you want to be doing the same work next year?

2. Do you like your career but feel you're in the wrong job?

3. Do you long for the weekends when you can work on hobbies or other interests?

4. Is there some other career choice that has always fascinated you?

5. Do you need to find something new that is fresh and creative?

6. Has your work become predictable and boring?

7. While change may seem scary, do you find yourself thinking a lot about switching careers?

*The road to happiness lies in two simple principles:
find what it is that interests you and that you can
do well, and when you find it, put your whole
soul into it—every bit of energy and ambition
and natural ability you have.*

JOHN D. ROCKEFELLER, III

8. Is there something you feel passionate about that you'd like to try if only you could figure out a way to earn a living?

9. Do you long for a way to make a contribution to the world and don't feel you can do it in your present work?

10. Does your life feel out of balance? (Too much work and not enough time for family, social, and personal time?)

If you answered "yes" to most of the questions, it's definitely time for a career change. If you're not clear about your next steps, your goal should be to *become clear*. Make an appointment with a career coach; take a class on the topic of career change; and/or begin to read some books on the topic of following your passion.

Make an inner decision that it's time for a change. Ask your intuition open-ended questions, such as, "What would I enjoy doing for work?" "What next steps can I take that will lead me in the right direction?" "Who can I talk with who will help me with these choices?" "What could I do that would help others and be fun for me?" As you go about your day, pay attention to any inner nudges or impulses from your intuition that point you in a new direction.

Following are some more questions to ask yourself that will help you begin to focus on getting in touch with your life purpose. As you reflect on this list and your answers, let the issue "How could I make a living at this?" rest for the time being.

We often put the cart before the horse. Deepak Chopra took note of this, saying, "When we seek money, or a good relationship, or a great job, what we are really seeking is happiness. The mistake we make is not going for happiness first. If we did, everything else would follow." When you can discover the "what" (you love), the Universe will help you with the "how" (to earn a living at it). You might want to get out your journal and write some answers to the following questions.

What are your gifts?

- What life achievements or accomplishments have made you feel proud?

- What abilities do you have that people praise?

- What tasks or skills come easily to you? Make a list of things you do well.

- What were you good at as a child?
- If someone were to give your eulogy, what contributions would they say you have made to the world?

*How wonderful it is that nobody need wait
a single moment to improve the world.*

ANNE FRANK

What are you passionate about?

- What do you do that makes you lose track of time?
- If you had enough money to take a year off, what would you do with your free time?
- Is there something you want to devote your life to?
- How can you help others by doing what you enjoy?
- If you could make one contribution to the world before you die, what would it be?
- What do you want to teach others?
- What excites or angers you most about our world?

What are your values?

- What matters most to you? Consider values like: autonomy, humanity, creativity, kindness, power, wealth, spirituality, knowledge, leadership, community, beauty, and intellectual pursuits.

- Think of someone you admire. What is it about the person's life that you appreciate? What values do you think he or she holds?

What's fun for you?

- Make a list of twenty, fifty, or a hundred things you love to do.

- How would you spend your ideal day?

- Do you enjoy doing things by yourself, with a partner, or with a team?

- What kind of setting do you like to be in? Are you an outdoor person or more comfortable behind a desk? Consider your surroundings when imagining your fun, ideal life.

As you look at your answers, are there any themes that emerged? Were there any "aha!" moments that caught you by surprise? Once you have your list of accomplishments, competencies, values, and passions there are a few more steps. The answer to the question "What's my life's purpose and how can I make a living at it?" may not come overnight. One of the qualities I believe we must develop on the spiritual path is that of patience. Napoleon Hill, the author of the classic book *Think and Grow Rich,* makes a good case for this very attribute when he states, "Patience, persistence, and perspiration make an unbeatable combination for success."

CHAPTER 16

Charting the Course to Your Prosperity

We come equipped with everything we need to experience a powerful life full of joy, incredible passion, and profound peace. The difficult part is giving ourselves permission to live it.

DEBORAH ROSADO SHAW

YOU KNOW THAT YOU FINALLY UNDERSTAND YOUR LIFE PURPOSE because the lights flash, the bells ring, and you experience a huge "aha!" moment, right? Not quite. The truth is usually much less dramatic. Your inner wisdom guides you through feelings of quiet joy, a nudge to try a new direction, a fleeting impression, or simply a desire for change. These are the clues to listen for and pay attention to.

What's next? How do you take action on the intuitive impulses you're experiencing? You may be able to figure out *what* you want, but *how* can you get there? This is the part that may make you feel anxious because your soul is requiring you to move out of your comfort zone, to try something new. You need to take action. Susan Jeffers writes in her wonderful book *Feel the Fear and Do It Anyway,* "We cannot escape fear. We can only transform it into a companion that accompanies us on all our exciting adventures. Take a risk a day—one small or bold stroke that will make you feel great once you have done it."

Faith is belief in the unseen, the quietly held
conviction that even though you can't imagine how,
at some time, in some place, in the right way, the
thing you desire will indeed come to pass.

DAPHNE ROSE KINGMA

When you make a commitment to follow your intuition, you will be guided step-by-step to an abundant life. The Universe is a big dream machine. As you allow yourself to become clearer about what kind of work you want, how you desire to use your skills to be of service in the world, and how much abundance you can allow into your life, the Universe responds. It will put the right people, circumstances, and ideas before you that will help you create the success you most desire. The Universe speaks to you through your intuition. It's your prosperity partner and will help you chart a course for the achievement of your heart's desire.

Following are some steps to help you begin to work with your intuition to take the right path toward a fulfilling and abundant life.

Ask for a dream before you go to bed at night. Write a brief note in your journal regarding your work and career thoughts. End your writing with a question to your higher self for an insightful dream. Some examples of questions you might ask are, "What kind of work would make me happy?" "What are the next steps for me to take regarding my work?" "I want to develop a career in ___. Is this the right path for me?" Say the question to yourself as you drift off to sleep. The next morning, before coming fully awake, write any ideas, impressions, or dream fragments in your journal. What career direction does your dream indicate? Take action on any insight you receive.

Look in the help wanted section of the newspaper. This is not as obvious as it first seems. Look with an eye to the job descriptions that leap out at you. Don't necessarily look at the jobs that make logical sense or the postings for which you have experience. Use your "intuitive" eye and see which ones make you think, "That would be fun!" Or, "I'd love to do that!" Cut them out or circle them and see if you can find a theme regarding their appeal. Do they involve a specific profession? Perhaps they call to the adventurer in you. Or, conversely, you might be drawn to them because you like the security they represent.

Talk to people who do the kinds of work you've identified as interesting. Call professional organizations and ask your friends if they know anyone in the field that you're interested in. Call your alumni association for names of people to whom you can talk. Ask your potential interviewee if he or she would be willing to spend some time with you either on the phone or in person. Have a list of questions to ask the person. Ask what it's like to do his job. Ask about his background and the experience needed for his work. What's a normal day like? What does he love and hate about his work? What advice does he have for someone like you who is interested in this work? Finally, is there anyone else he thinks it would be beneficial to talk with?

Your task at this time is to create a list of options. Look at every job that intrigues you and don't let your logical mind talk you out of it. Everything that you look at that elicits a sense of enthusiasm has a clue for you about the work that will ultimately make you happy, the work that is an integral part of your life purpose. You don't need to find the one "right" career or necessarily the one you'll do for the rest of your life. You'll find as you begin to pursue these areas of interest that doors will open and synchronicities will occur. This is the Universe responding and saying *yes!* to your plan of action.

As you gather information, your focus will naturally narrow. If you had to form a succinct statement of what you would love to do, how would you describe it?

Here's the way I would describe my life-purpose statement:

• I help people trust their inner wisdom so they create prosperous, joyful, and successful lives. I enjoy doing this through writing, coaching, teaching seminars, and talking to the media.

My financial planner defines his this way:

• I work with people who want to accumulate wealth by teaching them about sound financial planning. I do this by engaging in my passion for studying investment strategies and writing and speaking about them in a practical, easy-to-understand manner.

A friend who is a corporate recruiter says:

• I work with growing companies that need to find talented people so they can grow their business and become more profitable and successful.

A colleague who is an image consultant states her work like this:

• I help women dress for success so they look and feel like a million bucks.

As you begin to get a sense of what you're passionate about, try it out on a short-term or low-risk level, if possible. This might include taking a volunteer position, working as a consultant on a project basis, or taking a short-term, part-time position to see how your potential new career feels.

Learn to get in touch with silence within yourself,
and know that everything in this life has purpose.
There are no mistakes. No coincidences.
All events are blessings given to us to learn from.

ELISABETH KÜBLER-ROSS

Research indicates that at least 10 percent of the population has a strong aptitude in more than one area. If you're in this group, you'll be bored doing just one thing for very long. Consider the possibility that having several part-time or temporary jobs may be just the right fit for you.

Learn some new skills. This doesn't necessarily mean that you have to go back to college for an undergraduate or graduate degree. Many local colleges have adult learning programs and offer certificates in a course of study. Investigate internships or apprenticeships. My clients often report that these temporary positions allowed them to make the right contacts for the permanent work they were seeking.

As you're going through your list of ideas, remember that your decision may require a small step, not a huge leap. Quite often when you take a step forward, more information becomes available to you. Many people report that as they make an intuitive choice toward what proves to be a correct decision, events begin flowing more easily and effortlessly. Doors to opportunity open and synchronicity and coincidence begin to occur.

Think of the action steps I've listed in this chapter as well as others that may have occurred to you for your specific situation. Which one(s) are you drawn to? Is there one that leaps to your attention and captures your interest? You may experience a visceral charge about pursuing this course of action. Remember that a kinesthetic or physical sensation is one of the ways that intuition communicates.

Do you feel excited or passionate about one more than the others? This is one of the ways that intuition will point to the direction you should follow. Conversely, if a choice makes you feel depressed or discouraged, or you feel a great deal of resistance, you're ignoring a strong intuitive message if you continue on this path.

Also, remember to have fun with all of this. It may be scary if you're unemployed or just barely getting by financially. But your attitude of adventure, curiosity, and creativity can make all the difference. Author and speaker Robert Allen says, "Persistence, desire, and confidence are your wealth."

You've most likely heard the phrase "If you don't know where you're going, you'll probably end up there." With your intuition as your guide, you are beginning to chart a course to the life you were born to live.

CHAPTER 17

Thriving Through Life Transitions

First there is an ending, then a beginning, with an important empty fallow time in between. That is the order of things in nature. Leaf-fall, winter, and then the green emerges again from the dry brown wood. Human affairs would flow along similar channels if we were better able to stay in the current.

WILLIAM BRIDGES

MANY SELF-HELP ARTICLES MAKE THE PROCESS OF LIFE CHANGE and transition look easy.

Lose Your Job? Four Ways to Land a Six-Figure Job Next Week

Getting Divorced? Eight Dating Tips to Find the New Mr. Right

Broke? Visualize Your Way to Millions!

Often people fear that there's something wrong with them when they can't instantly jump back on their feet after a setback.

It seems easy for everyone else! Loretta LaRoche puts it so humorously when she says, "I'm always reminding people that the one constant you can count on is that things happen—and usually when you're not in the mood for them."

Experts on change and transition have various names for the stages of change we pass through. You have only to look at nature to see that all of life has ebbs and flows. There are seasons when plants and trees are flourishing, blooming, and growing, followed by a period where they regenerate, lying dormant for a while. We as humans are no exception to this cycle of nature. We have periods of time when we are filled to the brim with excitement and growth; we are achieving our goals, meeting with success at every turn. Life is fun, joy-filled, and amazing!

This phase is often followed by a phase in which we coast along smoothly. The job is going well, the marriage is happy, life is good. There may be a few bumps in the road at times, but most days we feel that we've finally found the secret to life. Blessed be! We are among the lucky ones.

It's tempting to think that if we do all the right things in the first two phases it will continue to be bliss all the time. However, this is usually not the case. The next phase is the one that very few people seem to like. *We begin to feel dissatisfied with what we've created.*

The most disquieting changes are the ones that appear out of the blue. Over a period of several weeks or months we find ourselves in the midst of unhappiness with our current life. What once gave us pleasure now seems boring. Nothing feels right. What gave us job satisfaction before now seems to leave us feeling empty and without meaning. Where we once leapt out of bed to begin our day, we now want to just turn over and go back to sleep. What's the point of it all?

I was having lunch with a colleague a few weeks ago. He spoke about how he'd accomplished so many of his goals and aspirations with the success of his company. He was justifiably proud of his achievements and yet he went on to say, "Why do I feel so sad? I should be happily enjoying everything I've created."

We've all experienced these third-stage life transitions. They're often characterized by feeling bored, restless, anxious, and on edge. I see these feelings as a call from your wise inner being indicating that change is needed. It's as if the Universe had conspired to tell you to look within, hibernate, lie fallow for a while and regain your strength for the next season of growth. The writer Charles C. West seemed to agree when he wrote, "We turn to God for help when our foundations are shaking, only to learn that it is God who is shaking them."

You'll never stand on the mountaintop,
unless you've stood in the valley.

RICK BENETEAU

If you're like most people, you respond by wishing the uncomfortable feelings would simply go away. What is the change that's needed? You may feel like you're in the midst of chaos and you can't find your way out. One client characterized this transition time as a "nightmare where she could see the doors that might lead to escape, but which door is the *right* door?" Making a bad decision could leave her worse off than before!

Unfortunately, clarity about the solution doesn't usually arrive at the same time as the problem. This makes you more scared. How will you support yourself if you have to alter your life in some as yet unknown way? "Dear God, why do I feel so confused and what is the meaning of all of this? Why can't I just go back to the way things were?" is the plea I frequently hear.

But all is not lost! Someone once said, "Confusion is that wonderful state that precedes clarity." Here are some ideas to consider in order to move wisely through this time of transition:

Difficulties are opportunities to better things;
they are stepping-stones to greater experience.

BRIAN ADAMS

Understand that you're not crazy. You just feel that way. As noted above, this type of life transition is likely to provoke some strong feelings, from fear to anxiety to peace and back again. Often your colleagues, friends, and family will try to make you feel better by offering solutions, quick fixes, and advice about what they feel you should do. Forgive them. It's difficult to watch someone in emotional pain (in this case you), and friends will always want to help.

Be patient. Sue Monk Kidd wrote in her wonderful book *When the Heart Waits*, "When you're waiting, you're not doing nothing. You're allowing your soul to grow up. If you can't be still and wait, you can't become what God created you to be." This transition period in your life is, in all likelihood, time limited. Practice saying the mantra "This too shall pass."

Get help with your finances. There's no use in sticking your head under the covers. Talk to a trusted friend or preferably a financial adviser. Get clear about how much money you have (or don't have) in order to get through this transition in a sane manner. Don't wait until you hit a financial crisis to figure this out. It only makes the stress worse. Is there a part-time job you can get or a possession you can sell? This is most likely a belt-tightening time. Make a list of services and things that you regularly buy. What can you cut back on to weather the crisis for a few months to a year?

Honor your grief. It hurts to let go of the old. Whether you've lost a friend, lost a job, or are just plain lost, you'll go through stages of grief. The most commonly mentioned are denial, bargaining, anger, depression, and acceptance. You won't go through them in order; some of these emotions will be stronger and last longer than others. The best way to manage them is to feel them and move through them. They're part of the healing process, although it may not seem that way at the time.

Join a support group. This might be a prayer circle, a job-seekers meeting, or a group of folks with an issue similar to yours. Tread carefully here. You want to come away from these sessions feeling better, not worse. There is a tendency in some of these sessions to complain, commiserate, and whine. Find one that is uplifting and makes you feel hopeful and connected to a supportive community. Friends are important during this time of change. You're fortunate indeed if you have longtime friends who care about you. If not, it's a good time to reach out and make new ones.

Manage your feelings. There are many transitions that you go through in a few months. You come out the other side feeling life is fresh and new and the turmoil of the change you've gone through seems almost forgotten. However, there are changes that leave a permanent mark on your soul. Losing someone—a child, a friend, a parent—there's nothing you can do to bring them back.

You may also lose something intangible—a sense of safety, hope, financial well-being, or a belief in your physical immortality. Whatever your loss, there is a part of this over which you have no control. The part that you *do* control is your attitude about it. Ask your inner wisdom the question "How can I find peace in this situation?" Listen for the answer. It will come and so will your serenity.

Talk to God. You can rail, yell, scream, and cry. God can handle it. Talk to God as you would to a good friend. Tell Him that you're scared and don't know what to do. Ask for insight. Ask for peace and be open to both when they come. The response may be presented through inner means such as your intuition. It may also come in an outer way. You may unexpectedly run into an old friend who has just the right thing to say, or you might find a passage in a book that leaps out at you as the answer you've been seeking.

Remember this, you are loved. You are cared about and surrounded by a loving presence at all times. You are not alone.

Volunteer your time. You may not have a lot of money to give away just now, but you probably have time. Volunteering helps the giver (you) as much as the receiver. Giving freely of your services may help you create needed structure in your life at a time when you most need it. It may also help you discover a new passion that will open the doors to a new career. Follow your heart. What do you love to do? Find a group or individual that needs what you're able to offer.

Transforming every "What will I do?" into
"What can I do?" fuels your fiscal creativity,
restoring a sense of peace as you pursue prosperity.

SARAH BAN BREATHNACH

Trust in a higher purpose. "Why am I going through this?" you ask. God knows! And I'm not being facetious. Asking that question when you're in the midst of any difficult situation doesn't usually provoke a satisfactory response. The Universe has a plan for your life. Have faith that the power that causes the sun to rise and set, the trees to bloom, and babies to grow, also knows how to grow your soul and a prosperous life for you. There is a master plan. The code to unlocking this plan lies in your ability to keep your heart open and listen to the voice of God within. Nothing else matters and all is unfolding perfectly. Trust the process.

CHAPTER 18

I Thought I'd Be Rich by Now

If you retired today I estimate you could live comfortably until about 2 P.M. tomorrow.

FINANCIAL PLANNER TO CLIENT

AH . . . RETIREMENT. MOST OF US WORK HARD AND DELAY GRATIfication through our entire lives to be able to get to the age where we can retire. What a magic word! Depending on your personality it may conjure up images of sleeping late, having time for your hobbies, puttering around the house, and catching up on the many books you've wanted to read. More adventurous folks might imagine travels to exotic places, community work, a vacation home, a new boat, and/or the prosperity and time to entertain friends.

If you're heading toward retirement, you have a lot of company; about seventy-six million baby boomers will be joining you. Many people assume they'll have more than enough money to retire and don't take the time to look closely at the numbers. For example, if you would like to retire at age sixty on a modest fifty thousand dollars a year and expect to live another twenty years, you'd need close to a million dollars in retirement savings.

A recent survey asked financial planners about the amount of money needed to retire successfully. The cold, hard facts were that these professionals believed that only 6 percent of Americans had saved enough for retirement. The U.S. Department of Health and Human Services reports that 96 percent of all Americans will retire financially dependent on the government, family, or charity.

That's rather sobering, isn't it?

Life would be infinitely happier if we could only be born at the age of eighty and gradually approach eighteen.

MARK TWAIN

Where does that leave you? If you're among the 96 percent who do not have enough to retire comfortably, you'll have to continue working. I can imagine a lot of moaning and groaning as you read this information. Does this mean that you'll have to work in a job you hate for the rest of your life in order to save enough for retirement?

I'm an incurable optimist (a friend once called me "pathologically positive!"), so you can trust me to put a more encouraging spin on this depressing news. Is it possible to retire well and

live a life you love without having a million dollars or more?!
I answer with a resounding "yes!"

Two thoughts come to mind immediately.

1. You can begin to do what you love now and find a way to
make a living at it. With this scenario, your life/work/retirement/
what-you-do-for-fun can all be one and the same thing. What a
novel idea!

2. In addition, you can determine what's important to you as
you grow older and find a creative way to fund that hobby, lifestyle, or interest.

Wouldn't it be wonderful to begin living your life now as if
you were already retired? What would that look and feel like to
you? Jerry Gillies, who wrote the book *Money Love,* defined prosperity as ". . . living easily and happily in the real world, whether
you have money or not."

Let's look at some options:

Work part-time or start your own business. There is an overwhelming amount of research that shows that people who have
an active interest in life and a support system of friends live
longer and healthier lives. The reality is that while some may
have the fantasy of sitting around in their rocking chair after
retirement, that lifestyle gets boring fast! Now is the time to
make the decision about what you've always wanted to do when
you were grown up and begin to take small steps toward actual-
izing that vision. My friend Marina always dreamed of being an
artist. She's partially funding her retirement by selling her oil
paintings in a growing number of galleries.

Perhaps you've always wanted to write a book, be an interior decorator, run a flower shop, work with disadvantaged kids, or volunteer for the Peace Corps. Whatever it is, you've probably had it in the back of your mind for years. Begin to see your retirement years as permission to do what you love. If not now, when?

Live well on less. Mortgages, automobiles, food, and clothing are where we spend a great deal of our money. How could you downsize and still enjoy a leisurely retirement? Perhaps a move from a house to a condo might be in your future? Inviting friends over for a home-cooked meal instead of to an expensive restaurant could be a great way to showcase your passion for cooking and save some money. Decide what your priorities are. If world travel is an absolute necessity in order for you to enjoy your retirement, what could you cut back on that would allow you to journey in style? When you identify what you want from life, begin to ask the question "How can I?" rather than "Why can't I?" Your intuition will begin to provide the answers.

I've had many clients and friends who view their retirement years as a time to do something out of the ordinary. Perhaps downsizing is really not your cup of tea; what are some ways you could continue your current lifestyle and not run out of money? Be willing to be creative! My client Mary Ellen was adamant about being able to both keep her dream house and travel in style. She ended up being able to do both by asking her best friend to be her roommate and traveling companion. They shared the mortgage and travel expenses and had a ball!

Take some risks and be willing to enjoy yourself. Retirement can be fraught with anxiety if you let it. It may seem like the height of absurdity to be asking yourself at fifty-plus years old, "What do I want to be when I grow up?!" However, you're never too old to change and grow!

As you approach retirement your future seems so unknown. You don't have a job to go to, kids to look after, or a boss to report to. Will you be healthy? Will you have friends and family around or will you be alone? No one can answer those questions for you. But how would you live your life if you knew you were to die in one year, five years, or more? Is there anything left undone? How would you like your obituary to read? I'd like mine to read, in part, "She lived her life passionately and enthusiastically, encouraging others to do the same."

Nobody grows old merely by living a number
of years. We grow old by deserting our ideals.
Years may wrinkle the skin, but to give
up enthusiasm wrinkles the soul.

SAMUEL ULLMAN

Perhaps this is the first time you haven't had a goal and you feel stuck and in a rut. Your intuition is always giving you clues about what to do next. Begin today by asking yourself, "What would be fun?" or "If I had an ideal life, I would . . ." What comes to mind when you ask those questions? Start small and keep taking the steps that your inner guidance indicates. Author and mythologist Joseph Campbell wrote: "Follow your bliss and doors will open where there were no doors before." Julia Cameron, author of *The Artist's Way*, put it like this: "Leap and the net will appear!" But at some mysterious point, you have no choice but to go. There is an irony in following one's bliss as one comes of age. There is never a perfect time and there will never be a more perfect time. Be willing to take a risk and go for it with gusto.

See the glass half full. What are the important things in your life? I heard a little girl interviewed on television following a family catastrophe. She said, "We may not be rich in money right now, but we're rich in friends and love." Feel the blessing of all that you *do* have in your life.

Abundance comes in so many forms, not just cold, hard cash. My mother-in-law considers herself very prosperous despite having what many would consider very little money. She lives surrounded by her children, grandchildren, and great-grandchilden. She's also loved by many members of the small retirement community in which she lives. People invite her out to meals, on trips, and on family outings. She is blessed by all the love she shares and it is returned in kind.

Gratitude invites abundance. Perhaps you have a close-knit family, good health, or a profitable skill. There is always a lot to be thankful for if you take the time to look. If you're really having trouble coming up with something you're grateful about, you might take comfort in the words of one woman: "I'm sitting here thinking how nice it is that wrinkles don't hurt."

Retirement planning is something to think about at any age. As you envision your older years, rank the importance of the following:

___ Having friends and family close by

___ Staying physically active

___ Making a contribution to society

___ Having unscheduled time for myself

___ Traveling alone or with friends

___ Continuing to work in my current career

___ Finding a new way to make a living

___ Devoting time and energy toward a hobby

___ Other (describe)

Look at the above list and take some time to evaluate your priorities. What are some ways that you can begin now to plan for a happy and fulfilling retirement? The change to a retired lifestyle doesn't need to take place abruptly at a specific age. The happiest folks are the ones who have enjoyed the *planning* of their retired years as much as the fulfillment of them.

CHAPTER 19

Creating a Divine Investment Plan

A lot of people will also urge you to put some money in a bank, and in fact—within reason—this is very good advice. But don't go overboard. Remember, what you are doing is giving your money to somebody else to hold on to, and I think that it is worth keeping in mind that the businessmen who run banks are so worried about holding onto things that they put little chains on all their pens.

MISS PIGGY

JOHN EARNS $325,000 A YEAR AS A SENIOR MANAGER AT A HIGH-tech firm and lives off his credit cards. Janice makes $28,000 as an administrative assistant at a health care facility and manages to save $3,000 a year toward her retirement. Here's a big secret—It's not how much you earn, it is how much you're able to keep. When you have a cash reserve you sleep easier, your self-esteem improves, and your financial cushion enables you to make healthy life choices. It's next to impossible to live a satisfying life when you're faced with huge credit card debt and an overwhelming mortgage. The debt disempowers you and diminishes your ability to make good decisions. Sound financial planning not only leads to peace of mind and spirit. It leads to financial security.

Many of my clients cite "lack of money" as the single biggest hurdle to overcome when contemplating a career change to do work they love. It becomes a vicious cycle. They hate what they're doing for work and thus spend more money buying things that they think will make them happier. They then save no money toward creating a nest egg that could help them transition into work they love. Does this sound familiar?

People say you should let your money work for you.
I'll work and let my money relax.

JERRY SEINFELD

No one was born knowing how to create a household budget, handle personal finances, or figure out investment strategies. Hopefully you learned some of it in school as well as from your family. However, if you're like most people, your money management strategy is to wait to win the lottery or pray for some other financial windfall that will make the debts go away and restore your financial sanity. On the other hand, anecdotal evidence suggests that if you don't have a financial savings plan you'll blow any windfall you receive and be back to where you were originally—or worse. Think about your own life experiences.

Have you ever received a raise or a bonus and immediately increased your spending to include it rather than put it into an investment account?

Imagine what it would be like to have ample reserves to do what you love. We're all able to tap into the Universal flow of abundance, but when we do, we need a vehicle for it to flow *in* to. For many, it flows into and *out* of their wallet! Just in case you were wondering, God did not intend that new credit card offer you received in the mail as the answer to your prayers. Financial management needn't be a dreary thing to understand and accomplish. Open your mind to discover fun and empowering ways to learn about it.

What's your learning style? There are three primary ways we learn things—by reading, listening, or doing. When you think about how you like to learn, what's your predominant mode? Your goal is to create a financial management system that works for you. Use your intuition. What feels most appealing? Would you pick up a book on personal finance? Listen to a tape? Go to an adult education class to learn the basics? Or just dive in and do your own version of "on-the-job training"? The latter might include learning a financial software program or talking to a friend who has a skill with money and money management.

Define the problem. I know most of you are saying, "The problem is that I just need more money!" It's easy to bury your head in the sand and continue to hope that the prosperity angel will visit you in your sleep, wave her magic wand, and "poof!" all your financial problems will be solved forevermore. It's probably not going to happen.

You're going to have to do what every financially stable person does to gain some clarity about his or her overall situation. I won't kid you and claim this is the fun part. It usually isn't, but it's a crucial step in your financial independence. Before you decide to skip this section because you're overwhelmed, ask yourself one question: "Would you rather have your money control you, or you control your money?" If you chose the latter, then get to work and gather all the facts and figures you need to answer the following basic questions.

What's your net worth?

If you're in debt, how much do you owe?

What is your current income?

What are your fixed expenses?

Other than fixed expenses, where is your money going?

What interest rates are you paying on mortgage, credit cards, and loan balances?

If they're high, what can you do to lower them?

Do you have a financial strategy to get out of debt and/or save money?

If not, what are two things you can do this week in order to begin the process?

Answering these questions may be the last thing you want to do. However, most people feel relief at having the facts and figures in front of them. The knowledge you gain will make you feel empowered and help you to understand what you need to do to gain control. You might even find things are not as bad as you imagined! If you aren't planning on how to manage money, then you aren't planning on being wealthy.

Brainstorm for financial solutions. The above exercise may have left you with the troublesome knowledge that change is needed. Don't despair! Use your intuitive mind to come up with some solutions. Give your inner guidance a challenge and ask, "What can I do that will allow me to create financial abundance right now?" A big sheet of paper and some colored pens will give you a creative edge. Now write down everything and anything that pops into your mind. Some of the items may be *moneymaking* ideas and others might be *money-planning* ones. Don't judge or critique your ideas at this stage. That just stops the flow of possibilities coming to your mind.

Here are some of the results of a brainstorming session that Rick and Carrie did in one of my classes:

Get a part-time job over the holidays.

Have a yard sale.

Offer to work overtime.

Refinance our house.

Call the credit card company and ask for a lower rate.

Pack bag lunches and eat out less frequently.

Sell some items on eBay.

Trade baby-sitting time with other parents instead of paying a baby-sitter.

Take a vacation closer to home this year.

Fix the car rather than buy a new one.

Be conscious of "small" items that are bought. Recognize that costs add up.

Make an appointment with a financial planner.

You might want to do this exercise every week for several weeks and see what new ideas your intuitive mind has come up with. Or simply keep the list on a wall and write down new items as they come to you.

I have enough money to last me the rest of my life,
unless I buy something.

HANNA HOLBORN GRAY

Now pick out the solutions that you're willing to live with. Cross things off the list that are impractical or that you know you're not going to do. It's easy to get overwhelmed. So, the next step is to prioritize the results you came up with. If you're doing this with a partner, divvy up the assignments and agree to talk about the results. If you're doing this on your own, you might consider asking a friend to help you with the brainstorming and to provide some emotional support while you're going through the process.

Keep the change! Here's a painless financial strategy that will help you see some immediate results. Keep the daily change you receive and put it into a jar or other container. At the end of three months or some other arbitrary time period, dump it out and count it. You'll be surprised how much this adds up to over a several-month period. Here's the key—don't spend it on a new extravagance. Put it into paying down your debt or into your investment account.

Invest your raise. Several years ago I raised my fees. I had been able to live on the income I was making, so I decided to sign up for an automatic deposit to my money market account each month. There were many things I *wanted* to buy with this money, yet the thought of putting it away gave me a bigger boost in confidence than any new outfit would bring. If you receive a raise or a bonus check, invest it. You probably won't miss it since it wasn't part of your regular budget. Think of it as your financial independence account!

Think rich—don't spend rich. Money used to burn a hole in my pocket. If I had fifty dollars, I could spend it in a few hours on a manicure, a book, and taking myself out to lunch. There's nothing wrong with treating yourself. I'm all in favor of that! However, part of having money is learning to save it. Money goes to and stays with people who love and take care of it. I needed to do that in a way that I wouldn't feel deprived and walk around saying, "I can't afford it," all the time.

Here's the game I learned to play: The game is guaranteed to help you control your impulse spending, boost your self-esteem, and build your self-discipline. Go to your bank and withdraw the largest single denomination bill that you feel comfortable carrying around with you. It might be twenty, fifty, a hundred dollars, or more. Fold it, put it into your wallet or pocket, and *don't spend it.* The last three words are the important part.

During the day, as you see things that you would like to buy, say to yourself, "I could have that. But I choose to save my money." Doesn't that feel infinitely better than the words, "I can't afford it?" (Remember, beliefs become reality!) I realized how often I bought things on impulse that I didn't really need. I had been using money as a little "pick me up" and it was wreaking havoc with my savings strategies.

Don't let shame, fear, or simple lack of knowledge stop you. Spending more than you earn is the recipe to certain financial disaster. Personal money management may seem quite overwhelming at first. But each step you take to learn about the topic and take action on your own situation will be one more step toward financial independence and, ultimately, a prosperous life you love.

CHAPTER 20

Have Courage as You Prosper

The whole point of being alive is to evolve into the complete person you were intended to be. I believe you can only do this when you stop long enough to hear the whisper you might have drowned out, that small voice compelling you toward the kind of work you'd be willing to do even if you weren't paid. And what do you do once you turn down the noise of your life and heed that call? You face the biggest challenge of all: to have the courage to seek your big dream regardless of what anyone else says or thinks. You are the only person alive who can see your big picture—and even you can't see it all.

OPRAH WINFREY

JENNIFER WALKED INTO MY OFFICE LOOKING TOTALLY DEJECTED. "I hate my job. I've been a bookkeeper for the same company for eight years and I'm so bored. It's the same thing, day in and day out." She continued this litany for several minutes, providing examples about how bad her job was, bemoaning the antics of her crazy boss, and the resulting dysfunctional office dynamics.

I was about to step in with a comment when she said something surprising. "I actually have a great idea for a new business. It's something I've wanted to do for years. I'm very excited about it. *I'm just too scared to try it.*"

I've heard her statement in various forms from so many people.

"I feel stuck."

"I don't know where to start."

"It probably won't work anyway."

"I don't want to let go."

"I'm waiting until I retire."

"I don't have the money."

"I'm scared."

Would it surprise you to know that most people are fearful before they do something new? I recently gave a talk to an audience of several hundred entrepreneurs. I asked, "How many of you were scared to death before you started your business?" Every single hand in the room shot up. It's anxiety producing to try something new. I asked a second question: "How many of you felt confident you had enough money when you started your business?" This time no one raised their hand. I asked my third and final question: "How many of you were certain your business idea would succeed?" This time one confident man raised his hand.

The stereotype of a successful entrepreneur is that of a confident self-starter who is bankrolled with venture capital money and a surefire idea. Nothing could be further from the truth.

Almost all the people in that room full of entrepreneurs had to overcome self-doubt and fear in order to begin the path that led to their new work. The feelings are the same for most of us, whether we choose to start our own business or make some other equally courageous change in our life.

Dreaming is easy. Acting on those dreams— saying to yourself, "Hey, wait a minute, I want this"—is another kettle of fish. It takes conviction and faith, even audacity. But consider a life without art, books, movies, design, or fashion. Every one of these things grew out of a dream pushing the boundaries of the possible.

MARTHA BECK

So if you're thinking about simply changing jobs, or even totally changing your career, you'll be besieged by the same internal questions. "Will I make enough money?" "Will I like the change?" "Will I be successful?" "How will I find clients or customers?" and "What if it doesn't work?" These are all perfectly valid questions! Understand, however, that there may not be satisfactory answers to them at first. That's where courage comes in! Eleanor Roosevelt understood this when she said, "You gain strength, courage, and confidence by every experience in which you really stop to look fear in the face. . . . You must do the thing which you think you cannot do."

Do you know what you are here to do? If not, here are some clues: What is the thing you feel passionate about? What work would you do even if you weren't paid for it? What do you read about or study in your free time? What are your hobbies? Is there a social system or injustice you see in the world that you feel strongly about changing? These are all signs from your inner guidance about a path to pursue.

What steps can *you* take to start down the path to your passion? Here are some tips:

Just begin. Perhaps you've gone to a career counselor, taken a personality test, and read innumerable self-help books and you still haven't identified your "purpose in life" or "life mission." You may be thinking too big and allowing yourself to feel overwhelmed. The quest for a joy-filled and prosperous life usually begins in fits and starts. Begin today to commit to making life a fun adventure rather than a search for deep meaning and hard cash. What are two new things you can do this week that are fun, outside the norm, and require a little courage? You'll likely discover, as many have, that as you do more of what you love, both the larger purpose and the prosperity begin to flow into your life.

Build your courage muscles. You know that you have to make a change in your life. Your finances are getting worse and you're feeling stuck in a dead-end job. Why can't you seem to make a fresh start? The excuse I've heard from many clients is "I'm scared." It would be wonderful if there were a "courage fairy" that could wave her magic wand and give you some of that precious commodity, but it probably isn't going to happen. Singer and speaker Jana Stansfield asks a wonderful question: "What would you do today if you were brave?" Developing courage is like building a muscle. The more you work at it and practice it, the stronger it gets. What are two things you've been telling yourself that you "should" do and yet haven't done because doing them makes you a little uncomfortable? Get out a package of Post-it notes, write those two things down, choose a deadline, and do them! You'll feel so much better when they're done. Plus, your courage muscles will be stronger!

Tune out the naysayers. There is at least one naysayer in everyone's life. You know them when you hear them. "It's a bad economy. Just make do with the job you have." "You'll never get ahead financially. You're bad at managing money." Or simply, "Play it safe. Don't take a risk." It takes courage to listen to and act on your own inner convictions. The most encouraging voice in your life should be your own. That's what counts. Finding your purpose and passion often means going against the well-meaning advice of your family and even your close friends. Take a leap of faith and trust in your dreams.

Move out of your comfort zone. Rome wasn't built in a day and your new life, prosperity, and career probably won't be either. But that's okay. Simply commit to begin.

Robert G. Allen is the author of the book *Multiple Streams of Income*. I once heard him speak at a convention. He held out his hands—about three feet apart—and said, "Everything you want is 'this far' outside your comfort zone." Get prepared to make changes in your life . . . and start making them! The Universe can't help you until you are willing to step out of your comfort zone.

Tune in to your intuition. Your inner voice is always with you providing wise guidance to assist you in creating the rich, wonderful, passionate life you deserve. Make use of it by asking it good questions. Asking, "Why can't I make money?" or "Why can't I get a better job?" is a setup for failure and despair. Instead, begin your day with questions like, "How can I create more abundance?" "What could I do for work that would make me happy?" "Where can I begin?" "What could I do today that would be a step in the right direction?" You get the idea.

No matter what degree of insecurity you are feeling,
a part of you knows there is a lot of wonderful
"stuff" within you just waiting to be let out
and now *is the perfect time for opening the*
door to the power and love within.

SUSAN JEFFERS

Ask open-ended questions with the expectation of insightful and helpful answers. Remember, these answers don't always pop into your mind fully formed. You may receive a gut feeling to call someone, and when you do, you receive a piece of information you need. Or you may have a fleeting impression about a course of study that turns out to be the perfect next step for a business you're thinking about starting. So, ask good questions, trust your gut, and grow a brand-new life. Here are three questions to get you started:

1. *What would you do today if you had the courage?*

Asking this question may provoke an immediate answer. If so, begin to take some small steps in this direction. Sometimes, the answer takes longer to come to you. Be open to any inner response over the next few days and weeks.

2. *What's the worst thing that could happen?*

Often our mind presents an entire worst-case scenario that seems destined to unfold if we have the audacity to go after our dreams. These imagined circumstances are usually highly unlikely, but it helps to be conscious of our fears.

3. *What's the best thing that could happen?*

It's important to give equal time to the positive side of things! Take some time thinking about this one! Once you define this and take your leap of faith you may be surprised how quickly positive change begins to occur!

You are here with a life purpose. You may not know the specific details of the mission. However, your intuition provides the "inner map" that guides you and is always giving you the correct coordinates to move you toward the grand design. This is your work and you are a pioneer on the trail to the lifelong unfolding of the assignment. Does it take courage? Yes! Will you have times when you feel lost and uncertain? Yes! Wherever you are on the path, you will always have a profound connection with God through your intuition. You are never alone. Have courage and follow your heart.

CHAPTER 21

God's Lottery

When the solution is simple, God is answering.

ALBERT EINSTEIN

IT'S CONFESSION TIME. WHO HASN'T DREAMED OF THE BIG WIND-
fall? Who among us hasn't had the thought, at one time or
another, "If only I could win the lottery, I would . . ."

Quit my job

Volunteer

Buy a house by the beach

Travel around the world

Help the disadvantaged

Live the life I've always dreamed

And on and on

I have news for you. *You may have already won!* Do I sound like those awful direct-mail pieces you receive in the mail? Let me explain . . . God does have a lottery of sorts. He doesn't dole it out like Santa Claus, according to who's been naughty and who's been nice. He doesn't always give it out all at once like a traditional lottery might. You don't have to do anything to prove that you're worthy of it. You already are! Most important, it doesn't always come in the form of money. Huh?

I believe that the Universe is a vast magnificent system of abundance. The way we receive this wealth is through ideas, thoughts, and opportunities. It also comes through connections to people, events, and circumstances. God doesn't just come out of the heavens and say, "You there! Good job! Here's a check for a thousand dollars." Instead, we are given ideas to grow a profitable new business, a job where we can learn new things and be able to contribute to our community. The wisdom of the Universe also provides amazing synchronistic events that give us exactly what we need, often without cash.

I'll give you an example. Several years ago my husband and I wanted to take a trip to Florida in the midst of a very cold and snowy New England winter. We were in what I euphemistically call a "belt-tightening mode," having just put an expensive addition on our home. We were feeling a little down, because we'd decided that the combined cost of travel, lodging, and food was a little more than we felt comfortable spending. I'm usually the incurable optimist and secretly decided that we were going anyway. I figured that God had simply not made the arrangements yet!

About a week before the date I had planned, I received a call from a good friend who lives down there. She said the company she worked for owned several condos usually reserved for visiting customers. Quite unexpectedly, one became available the week we wanted to be there. "Would you and Gary like to come down and stay here?" I called my travel agent, got a great price on air-fare, and had a wonderful week's vacation in a luxurious condo.

Inside your life energy, personality, and mind is an oscillating molecule of infinite goodness, the divine Light; the Christ consciousness. If you align to that infinity within you, you will always have energy. There is no limit to the amount of the God Force you can have.

STUART WILDE

"Abundance is not something we acquire. It is something we tune into," states Wayne Dyer. Did I win a multimillion-dollar lottery? Obviously not, but as Dyer implies, I believe I had tapped into a Universal energy that had worked to my benefit to bring me exactly what I needed and wanted.

What about you? Close your eyes for just a moment and think of the turning points in your own life. Someone once said, "Coincidences are God's way of remaining anonymous." Was there a time when you were down on your luck and some unexpected event occurred to turn the tide for you? God's hand is in the smallest details of your life. Learn to look for and expect His miracles. When you keep your heart and mind open and expect the best, opportunities for abundance abound.

Let me give you another example. Several months ago, I spoke with Melinda, a young woman from South America. She was in this country on a scholarship, in debt, and struggling to support her thirteen brothers and sisters, and a sick mother in the ailing economy of Colombia. She was feeling rather desperate because she had decided that she hated her course of study. She realized that she had chosen it only because it was something that was offered to her and she felt she couldn't turn it down. What she really wanted to do was go to medical school.

You can imagine from the circumstances I've described that this was a virtually impossible financial stretch. She prayed to God to win the lottery so she could study medicine in Texas. I spoke with her about my theory that the Universe often creates mysterious ways to give us what we need if we are open to it.

A few weeks later she called me again and said two wonderful things had happened. She had been serendipitously introduced to a woman who handles financial aid for the Texas college system. This woman was more than happy to help Melinda find sources of funding for her medical education.

Melinda had also followed an impulse to call a friend she hadn't spoken to in a long time and mentioned her desire to move to Texas. The friend exclaimed that most of her extended family lived there. Later in the week, Melinda received a call from the friend's Texas family saying they would welcome her with open arms and she could live with them as long as she needed.

Another client, Daniel, called me after he was laid off from a job and his wife of twenty-five years had filed for divorce. This was not an easy time for him and yet he was determined to make the most of it. He expressed a desire to start his own company in the same industry that he had just left. He had been a successful salesman for many years but always felt that he could make more money on his own. He had a small nest egg left from the sale of his home but was understandably anxious about the possibility of losing it all on a bad business venture.

Daniel made the same joke I've heard many times, "Do you see me winning the lottery?" We talked about what he wanted. I asked him about his hopes and dreams for the business. He had a very well thought out plan that he articulated with great enthusiasm. I told him about the "God's lottery" idea and he laughed and hoped he could win it.

Are you discouraged? Hold on—because your
encouragement check is in God's postal system.

LANE PALMER

Only a week later he phoned. His message said, "Call me. You won't believe what just happened." When I reached him he described a whole series of events that were better than money in the bank! Another company had just bought out his major competitor. The new company intended to close the rival division. When the company's customers found out, they began calling Daniel's fledgling firm in droves, wanting to work with him. Daniel found his one-year goals manifesting within one month of starting his business. On top of that, he was able to hire some of the rival division's best employees, who were all eager to work for him.

If you contemplate these stories for even half a moment, you realize that no earthly lottery compares to God's lottery. With the former, you get money. With the latter, you get work you love, joy, fulfillment, circumstances that support your growth and well-being, and the pleasure of being of service in the world. You are entitled to these blessings. They are yours to enjoy.

What's needed is to shift your focus from scarcity and begin to open up to the possibilities that life and God can afford. While this sounds easy, it requires patience, practice, and faith. Sometimes we pray for a quick fix from our small perspective of life and don't allow ourselves to look at the bigger picture. The Universe has infinite resources to provide you with the abundance and wherewithal you deserve.

You are part of a larger reality. Do you think that God would have given you a life purpose, a passion, a mission, and not given you the means to do what you have come here to accomplish? It takes creativity and a willingness to look outside the box in order to find those resources. Be open to the Universe of possibilities.

CHAPTER 22

Kicking the Worry Habit

Ninety-eight percent of what I worried about never happened.

MARK TWAIN

I HAD A RECENT CONVERSATION WITH MY FRIEND CATHY, WHO IS quite wealthy by most people's standards. She said she was feeling poor and exclaimed, "I worry about whether I'll be able to take my trip around the world this summer." This may seem laughable to most of you reading this and yet her fear and worry were palpable. When we worry, we picture a negative result in our mind. It feels very real to us and our emotions begin to go along with this image we hold. We begin to feel fear, anxiety, and hopelessness. Even if the imagined concern never happens, the worry has taken its toll.

Edward M. Hallowell, M.D., who wrote a book titled *Worry: Hope and Help for a Common Condition,* states, "Worry is amazingly common. At least one in four of us—about 65 million Americans—will meet the criteria for an anxiety disorder at some point in our lifetime." Unlike my friend Cathy, most of us worry about issues that are closer to home. Can I pay my mortgage this month? What if my husband loses his job? What if my parents need long-term care? I've maxed out my credit cards and don't know how I'll ever pay them off. Help!

When you worry excessively you become afraid to take risks or try something new. Chronic worry steals your prosperity. It robs you of peace of mind. It cheats you out of living a full, rich, and abundant life, a life you deserve. You begin to lose hope that things won't change until your situation does. Indeed, you feel hopeless.

Ask yourself, "What's the worst that can happen?"
Prepare to accept it. Then improve upon the worst.

DALE CARNEGIE

Author Melodie Beattie writes, "What if we knew for certain that everything we're worried about today will work out fine? What if . . . we knew the future was going to be good, and we would have an abundance of resources and guidance to handle whatever comes our way? What if . . . we knew everything was okay, and we didn't have to worry about a thing? What would we do then? We'd be free to let go and enjoy life."

How do you begin to make the change from being an anxious worrier to being a person who is confident about your choices and full of faith about your future? How do you, as Beattie encourages, "let go and enjoy life"? Here are some tips to help you make the transformation:

Observe your worry. What are your most common "worry thoughts"? Over a period of several days, begin to write them down. Pay close attention to any thoughts or phrases that really grab you and disturb your well-being. Perhaps you have broad anxieties about "never getting ahead," or more specific ones like "what happens if my car breaks down and I can't afford to fix it?" Many people are not even aware that they worry. They just experience a state of generalized anxiety. Awareness of your worry habit is the first step toward the transformation to peace of mind.

Shift your thinking. After you've had a chance to analyze the pattern of your worrying, you may begin to see a theme emerge. Perhaps you'll recognize a deeply held belief that you're "not lucky" or that you'll always be poor. Begin to examine those thoughts. How could you shift those opinions so that they're more positive? I'm not suggesting that, like Pollyanna, you just wish them away. I'm advocating replacing the chronic worry thoughts with ones that create a more peaceful mindset. When you find yourself beginning to worry, try one of these phrases instead: "Things have a way of working out." "Most of the things I worry about never happen anyway." "I'll get through this tough time."

What are the expressions that make you feel better? One positive thought at a time can gradually shift the balance of your thinking from depressing to encouraging. Write down your positive thoughts and put them in a prominent location.

Distract yourself. If you've worked up a good head of steam worrying about your financial affairs and thought-shifting seems laughable, distract yourself! Forcibly take your mind off the thing you're anxious about. Get out of the house. Call a friend. Go to the movies. Pet your cat. Take the dog for a walk. Talk to a neighbor. Read a good book. Go to the gym. Plan a special dinner for you and your mate. Play with your kids. Think about some fun activities for the upcoming weekend. What works for you?

I believe God is managing affairs and that He doesn't need any advice from me. With God in charge, I believe that everything will work out for the best in the end. So what is there to worry about?

HENRY FORD

Get creative. I've talked to people about how they handle bouts of overzealous worrying and heard some funny but effective techniques. Cliff has a worry box. He writes all of his anxieties on a piece of paper and sticks them in a box on his bookshelf. Once a year he pulls them all out and is delighted to discover that 99 percent of the things he's written about never happened. Erica exaggerates her worries and captivates me with hysterical worst-case scenarios. She finds that if she can laugh about her concerns, she can more easily let them go! Kate has a huge "worry doll" in her office. If all else fails, she tells the doll it's *her* turn to worry! It serves as a reminder that she can put her worries away for the time being. What's a creative way for you to handle your concern?

Take action. It was Will Rogers who said, "Even if you're on the right track, you'll still get run over if you just sit there." Worry can emotionally paralyze you if you let it, and nothing cures worry faster than taking action. Sit down for a moment and write down the biggest concern you have. Maybe it's the one that wakes you up at 3 A.M. or the one that niggles at the back of your mind throughout your workday. Now quickly list four— and only four—things that you can do to begin to create a solution. Your list might include calling a friend to talk over the issue, or making an appointment with a financial planner to get some facts about your situation. Perhaps you could take a class to learn about managing your finances better. These tasks do *not* have to be big. In fact, the smaller the better, because that increases the likelihood you'll actually *do* them! Write your list now.

Life's up and downs provide windows of opportunity to determine [your] values and goals. Think of using all obstacles as stepping-stones to build the life you want.

MARSHA SINETAR

Move your body. Exercise in any form will reduce anxiety, because it induces the production of endorphins, the body's natural tranquilizers. Choose an activity that's fun for you to do. There are so many to choose from—yoga, walking, swimming, playing tennis, dancing, bicycling, to name a few. What did you enjoy doing when you were a child? That may give you a clue about what sport to pursue as an adult. Exercise promotes sleep, reduces our tendency to overeat, helps us concentrate, and assists us in controlling worry. The United States surgeon general reports that physical activity "reduces symptoms of anxiety and depression and fosters improvements in mood and feelings of well-being." Obviously, exercise isn't going to make your financial problems go away. What *will* happen is that you'll feel better, experience less anxiety, and have more energy. All of these will contribute to a generalized well-being that leaves you open to prospering messages of abundance from the Universe.

Pray or meditate. Talk to God about your financial concerns. There are all kinds of formal prayers beseeching the Divine for abundance. However, I'm a big believer in simply talking from your heart. "God, I'm worried about being able to pay the bills this month. I know there are many ways you can help me work this out to create abundance. I place this in your hands." The Reverend Dr. Robert H. Schuller claims that "There are 365 verses in the Bible that begin with the words 'Fear not.'" Many religions and spiritual practices encourage us to put our fears in the hands of a higher power. Say whatever is in your mind or heart, but affirm what you (hopefully) now know to be true, *that prosperity is your divine birthright.* If simply talking with God feels foreign to you, read the Prosperity Prayer in chapter 9. Many people find it difficult to still their mind enough to meditate effectively. It's particularly hard when you're in a phase of anxiety. If this is true for you, simply sit for no more than five minutes and say a comforting phrase or phrases out loud or to yourself, such as: "The Universe is abundant." "God provides all that I need." Or, "I let go of fear and worry and know that everything will work out fine."

If worry is a big issue for you, get out your journal and write your thoughts on the following questions:

What do I worry about most?

What is the worst thing that could happen?

What are five things I could do to prevent that from happening?

What strategy can I implement the next time doubt and worry begin?

When you become conscious of your worries and have a plan of action to handle them, you'll find they begin to dissipate. The anxiety you used to feel will be replaced with a sense of freedom and tranquility.

CHAPTER 23

Learn to S.O.A.R.

The universe is transformation; our life is what our thoughts make it.

MARCUS AURELIUS

I THINK OF MONEY AS A GAME. I OFTEN WAIT IN DELIGHTED ANTICIpation to see the latest way that the Universe will deliver abundance to me. It always does and I am eternally grateful. I am often in awe of the miraculous and creative ways that it arrives.

I have been working with the techniques in this book for over twenty years. I've formed a conscious habit of being clear about my goals and desires and an awareness of my thoughts, beliefs, and emotions. Because of this practice, I usually create what I want. Sometimes it takes awhile to arrive and at other times I see evidence of the manifestation immediately.

I've noticed as I've been writing this book over the past several months that I had some hidden resistance preventing me from having what I would consider *more than enough* money. I suspect it's something that many of you experience, too. Let me give you an example.

My husband and I recently decided we needed to purchase a new mattress for our bed. If you've gone shopping for one lately, you know they're not inexpensive. A moderately priced mattress set costs around seven hundred dollars. We have that money in our checking account and yet I found myself feeling rather depressed at the prospect of spending it. Throughout the day I'd find myself running numbers in my mind. If I bought the mattress, then I wouldn't be able to buy something else. I kept visualizing the seven hundred dollars subtracted from the total in our account and I could feel my spirits begin to sink.

Appreciation can make a day, even change a life.
Your willingness to put it into words
is all that is necessary.

MARGARET COUSINS

I finally realized that what I was doing was "scarcity visualizing." I was imagining less money and making up this story in my mind that what was in our checking account was our only source of money. You may have a different version of what I was doing. You may imagine that you have to put this purchase on your credit card and envision the difficulty you'll have paying the ever-growing Visa or MasterCard bill. You might simply say to yourself, "I have to make do with my old, lumpy mattress because I'm really poor." You might have the image of sleepless nights on this uncomfortable bedding in your head and thus reinforce your state of poverty.

As I became aware of my own inner thinking process while contemplating this purchase, I heard a different inner voice. It's the voice I connect with my intuition. I heard, "Lynn, you need to soar." That didn't make any sense to me other than being a nice little saying. I dismissed it. Of all people, I should know better than to do that with intuitive messages. My only excuse was that I was caught up in negative thinking!

I often find that when you ignore a true piece of inner guidance, it comes back in a louder, or possibly different, form. I call these "intuitive nudges." I was definitely getting "nudged" by the phrase "You need to soar." I finally sat down to meditate and tried to clear my mind. Remember that intuition often presents itself as a symbolic image or picture. When I finally allowed myself to get into a state of receptivity I saw a little sign in my mind's eye. It said:

SOAR . . .

Stop—Observe—Adjust—Receive

Over the course of the next few days, bits and pieces of a powerful prosperity technique began to form in my mind. Here's what I learned:

Stop

The first step in breaking any habit is to be aware that you're doing it. Catch yourself in the act of your scarcity-thinking pattern. What do you consistently say to yourself? Here are some common ones that I hear from clients. "I can't afford it." "I'll never get ahead." "I'm stuck in this low-paying job." "I don't know how I'll manage to pay the bills this month." "I feel like I live on the edge all the time." Or simply, "I'm *so* stressed!"

Understand that what you are saying to yourself may *appear* true to you. Up until now these negative thoughts were the message you were sending to the Universe. They were the beliefs you hold manifesting as reality. Remember that the Universe always says "yes." Are these thoughts the ones you want affirmed? My guess is that they're not. So the first prosperity key is to Stop making them!

Observe

Simply observe the comments you've been making. Don't beat yourself up about these thoughts. Examine the nature of the negative thoughts. Is there an underlying theme that you observe? This could be a belief in your lack of self-worth, a concern about your money- or time-management skills, a chronic pessimistic approach to life in general or money in particular.

Be gentle and kind during this stage. If you heard a loved one saying the self-defeating words listed in the "Stop" section, you'd probably want to rush in and provide some comfort and encouragement. Don't put a lot of time, energy, and focus on *why* you have these beliefs. Simply ask yourself, "Are these statements something I want to continue creating in my life?" The answer, most likely, is no.

Appreciate

You're aware of the negative thoughts; you've managed to stop them and you've paid attention to their content with gentle observation. The key now is to shift your focus off what you *don't* want and put it onto an idea or thought that feels good. Research shows over and over again that gratitude and appreciation create abundance. Motivational speaker Tony Robbins says it best. "When you are grateful, fear disappears and abundance appears."

When you are discontent, you always want more,
more, more. Your desire can never be satisfied.
But when you practice contentment, you can
say to yourself, "Oh yes—I already have
everything that I really need."

DALAI LAMA

If you look, you'll find many things to be appreciative about in your current life. They don't need to be about money or prosperity, or related to your current financial status. Here are some examples from my own life today:

My neighbor stopped by with freshly made cookies.
     It's really nice to have people who are so thoughtful
     in my life.

I took a break from writing this afternoon and enjoyed
     a long walk around some gardens a few minutes' drive
     from my house.

My son turned twenty-one years old today. It was nice to
have him over for dinner last night and I appreciate
what a great guy he is.

My husband made a cup of tea for me and brought it up
to my office. It made me feel cared for.

The intention of the Appreciation phase is to help you shift
your thoughts and feelings away from "poor me" and toward
gratitude. The change in focus assists you in becoming a vibrational match to what you want to create in your life. That is,
more ease, money, joy, and peace.

Receive

Here's the tricky part. "Receive" doesn't mean that having completed the "S-O-A" part of SOAR that money will now magically
appear in your wallet or show up in your bank account. Rather
it's an *attitude* of *reception*. It's an opening up to the abundance
that is God within you and the Wisdom that fills the Universe.
It's a mind-set of releasing fear and allowing faith.

When I shift into "Receive" mode I take a deep breath and in
my mind's eye envision my arms outspread to receive. I feel my
heart open, my breathing calm, and a sense of peace come over
me. Then I know, deep down, that I'm safe. I have enough *right
now,* today. Everything is okay. I trust in a power greater than
myself to provide me with all that I need in order to do the work
that I am here to do.

CHAPTER 24

Cheap Dates Can Be Fun

The safest way to double your money is to fold it over twice and put it in your pocket.

FRANK MCKINNEY HUBBARD

WHEN YOU THINK ABOUT HAVING UNLIMITED WEALTH, YOU MAY find yourself fantasizing about new cars, travel to exotic locations, new electronic gadgets, designer clothes, and fabulous homes. Have you ever planned for a trip months or even years in advance? You look forward to it, read brochures on the area, and think about the fun you'll have while you're there. Then, you're there! You have a glorious time, see all the sights, and you're home again a week or two later. You're back to your normal life and back to paying off the credit card debt incurred on your trip.

It's the same thing with a new car, the latest fashion outfit, or the most up-to-date computer. It all becomes old very rapidly. The quick thrill you experienced at being able to purchase it and own it may have been the extent of the pleasure it gave you.

While there's nothing wrong with buying expensive things, the key to creating the wealth you want and deserve is not necessarily in making more money; it's in keeping the money you make. One client added up the cost of her "luxury" expenditures over a two-month period and then figured out how many hours she worked to finance them. She was appalled at the ratio. She became determined to have fun, adventure, and excitement in her daily life while saving money.

My friend Barbara and I met for lunch in Boston's Italian North End last summer. We had picked our destination from a review in the local paper. As we walked down a narrow street toward the restaurant, people were speaking Italian all around us. We rounded a corner and came upon a group celebrating the Feast of St. Anthony with a parade, music, food, and merriment. Barbara looked at me and laughed, "You know, I feel like we're in Rome!" We had a great lunch and a wonderful afternoon, and she was right.

Resolve not to be poor.
Whatever you have, spend less.

SAMUEL JOHNSON

Her fantasy got me to thinking. There's nothing wrong with wanting the trips, cars, homes, etc. If you have the money to enjoy all these things without going into debt or blowing all your savings, go for it! But how often do we overlook what's right in our own backyard, town, or region? There's so much that the Universe provides for our enjoyment that is free or inexpensive. With that realization, I became the "Cheap Date Queen" and was determined to find ways to incorporate fun into my *daily* life.

Your life doesn't have to be just about getting up, going to work, coming home, getting dinner, helping the kids with their schoolwork, and going to bed again. Fun and enjoyment needn't be relegated to once or twice a year vacations or the temporary high from buying some new expensive gadget.

What's fun for you? Is it cooking for friends, exploring a new place for a walk, playing a game of catch with the kids in the neighborhood, or going to the theater? Perhaps this is a time to catch up on your reading or to take a class. Oprah Winfrey writes, "[If you pay attention] to the times you've felt most joyous, most fully engaged, most connected with yourself and others—you'll always be guided to the next best place. The only courage you need is to follow your passion." Your sense of joy is the very thing that may open up those much-needed next steps to the rich life you deserve!

Take a moment to remember the last time you really had fun.

What were you doing?

What made it fun?

Were you with good friends, family, or alone?

Did the amount of money you spend relate to the
    amount of fun you had?

What are the top seven things you love to do in your
free time?

If you were to take an absolutely fabulous vacation,
where would you go and what would you do?

How could you be creative and replicate that vacation
inexpensively?

Here are some ideas about how to have fun on your very own
cheap dates:

Check out your local theater, opera, or symphony groups.
High schools, colleges, and many towns have wonderful con-
certs and Broadway shows at a much lower price than the real
thing. During the summer months, your town might offer a
"concert in the park" series. Grab some bread, cheese, and fruit
and experience an evening of fun under the stars. Better yet, ask
some friends along to join you.

Be a tourist and explore your own town or region. I live in
New England, a place where people from all over the world come
to visit. I'm blessed to be in a location within easy driving to six
states. However, it shocked me one day to realize that I had done
very few tourist-type things in my own neck of the woods. How
about you? What about sightseeing in your own city?

If you've determined that frequent eating out is eating into
your budget, consider going out for breakfast or lunch instead
of dinner. When my husband and I travel, we often make our
lunch the "big meal" of the day and have appetizers or salad for
dinner. We also have a standing Sunday morning "date" at the

local diner for breakfast. It's a wonderful ritual that allows us to catch up on the past week and plan for the next.

Feeling lonely or just want to make some new friends? Consider joining or starting a neighborhood book club. I've been part of one for over five years and it's a source of a lot of laughter and sense of community. Other friends we know created a "Supper Club." A group of seven to eight people takes turns hosting a potluck dinner at each other's homes.

A man is rich in proportion to the number
of things he can afford to let alone.

HENRY DAVID THOREAU

Volunteer! What do you love to do as a hobby? Is there a way you could share that talent with a local nursing home, hospital, day care center, or other nonprofit organization? You may also be surprised at how frequently something you offer for free can open the door to paid opportunities.

Picnics are a great alternative to eating out. I work from home and in the warmer months, I often pack a sandwich or some leftovers and go sit by a waterfall a short drive from my house. Put the family in the car and bring a picnic with you to the beach, or put it in a backpack and plan to eat at a particularly scenic point along a trail.

Pick your own vegetables and fruits. I have pleasant memories of picking strawberries with my parents as a kid. My mom and

I would make strawberry jam together. We'd also freeze some of the berries and enjoy strawberry shortcake during the winter months that followed.

What did you love to do when you were a kid? Go to the local playground and swing on the swings. Grab a friend and take turns on the teeter-totter. Start up a game of ball with some neighbors. Play miniature golf, throw a Frisbee, or go bowling. You're never too old to be a kid again!

If you're embarrassed to do kid things by yourself and you don't have small children, consider "renting" a kid for the day. If there's a local event for children that you think would be fun, ask your neighbor's kids or your nieces and nephews to go with you. They may just help to remind you how to be a child again.

Go on a factory tour. They're usually free. They're also fun and very educational. It's fascinating to watch how something is made, built, or packed. I've been on tours for companies that make chocolates, jams and jellies, potato chips, and ice cream. (Hmmm . . . notice a theme here?)

Go to local church, craft, or community fairs. They're fun and a terrific source of inexpensive, original, and creative gifts for holidays and birthdays. They often have entertaining games and amusements for the kids, as well.

Watch a sunrise or sunset. Everyone talks about walks on the beach and enjoying the sunset. When was the last time *you* took the time to take pleasure in nature's abundance?

Play millionaire for a day. Get dressed up in your nicest clothes and drive to an upscale neighborhood and check out the real estate. Saturday and Sundays are the best. That's when there are likely to be open houses. Walk through as if you're a potential buyer. Check out the kitchen and open the cabinets and the refrigerator, walk out onto the deck and through the living room, bedrooms, and family room and imagine what it would be like to live there. This is a great tool for helping you to visualize your dream home.

Don't stop there! You need furniture for that house. Check out an expensive shopping area. Sit in some of the costliest sofas; put your feet up on one of the reclining chairs. Check out Jacuzzis and sound systems and learn about oriental rugs. If you can get your mate to play along, discuss your color schemes and decide where you would put each piece of furniture in your dream house. One caveat to this cheap date is to make it clear that you're "just looking." Don't waste a salesperson's time if you're not going to buy.

I am beginning to learn that it is the sweet, simple things of life which are the real ones after all.

LAURA INGALLS WILDER

Take a class. What would you love to learn about? My dream is to take a cooking class in Provence in the south of France. Meanwhile, I've taken classes on how to make croissants from a local chef, another seminar on growing a windowsill kitchen herb garden, and a brush-up class on French for tourists. Many towns have inexpensive adult education courses, and colleges often allow you to audit classes for free or a small fee.

So what's your favorite way to have fun? I'm sure you can think of many more than the ones I've listed here. One of the many secrets to creating an abundant life is to enjoy the one you have here and now. If not, you'll end up like the author Colette, who exclaimed, "What a wonderful life I've had! I only wish I'd realized it sooner."

CHAPTER 25

Failing on the Way to Success

A setback can lead us to a better place—if we just let it.

ANNE WILSON SCHAEF

I WAS READY FOR A CHANGE IN MY LIFE. I WAS GETTING BORED WITH my job. I was only twenty-four and seeking a new adventure. I heard about a position with a new company in upstate New York, applied for it, and went for an interview. A week later I received the call from the company's vice president offering me the job. I gave notice to my current boss, packed up my apartment, and said good-bye to my friends. A few days later my cat and I were on our way. Things promptly went downhill from there. I worked for the company for two months and then it went out of business.

I was in a new city with no friends. I had very little money as the move and the setup of a new apartment had taken the small nest egg I had accumulated. I was devastated, lonely, and scared. "How did I get to be a failure so early in my life?" I asked myself. I stayed in that panicked state for months, unable to break myself out of the inertia and anxiety that enveloped me.

If you could have read my mind during that time it was a litany of fear-based thoughts. "I don't have what it takes." "I'll be broke and on the street." "I don't have enough education or experience to get another job." I couldn't seem to get myself mobilized to do even a minimal job search. I had a vague idea that I wanted to "help people" and was interested in all things spiritual but that information did not easily lead to a job search action plan! The only thing I could think to do was pray and hold on to what felt like a feeble intuition that everything would be okay.

The answer to my prayer came one morning when I picked up a local paper and saw a class, scheduled for that evening, on how to develop intuition. This topic had always been a passion of mine and I decided to go. The short version of the story is that after attending the session, I realized I was very good at "giving readings" and that I might be able to make a living that way. I also met a wonderful woman who, upon hearing I was new in town, wanted to throw a party and introduce me to her friends.

The convergence of the party and the announcement of my new "occupation" resulted in people making appointments with me. My new work was born. I came to see that my move and being laid off from my job was, in fact, a gift. Anne Wilson Shaef, author of *Meditations for Living in Balance*, writes, "What we perceive as a failure may simply be our inner being's way of telling us that we are ready to move to a new level of growth." I had been given a new career, a new lease on life, and like-minded friends, and I was now embarking on a journey for which I had true passion.

Are you in the midst of a perceived failure? Perhaps you've been laid off from your job, you're on the brink of bankruptcy, or you're going through an acrimonious divorce. While you may wish otherwise, these situations are painful and difficult. They require that we face our deepest fears of inadequacy, lack, and failure. It's often during these difficult times that we turn to God and deepen our faith and spiritual connection. Author Paul Brunton states it this way: "When every situation which life can offer is turned to the profit of spiritual growth, no situation can really be a bad one."

Nobody escapes dark times. It's not a matter of if we'll have them; it's just what we'll do when we do have them. If our goal is to avoid the darkness, we never really find the light. If our goal is to avoid pain, then we never really find true joy. God can work most powerfully in our lives while we willingly spend time in darkness.

MARY MANIN MORRISSEY

Our intuition is connected to a wiser part of us that sees the larger picture of our lives and knows what we need to learn in order to move ahead on our journey in this life. Patience, trust, and faith are required after life hands us an unexpected blow. You were not sent here to fail. It may be hard to trust that the Universe knows what it's doing and yet that may be the path of least resistance. You need to go with the flow and know that there is a new and wonderful life for you just waiting to be born.

Tough times never last. When you are experiencing a setback you fear you'll be in it forever. However, generally speaking, most of life's painful disappointments are relatively short-lived. It's important to remember that we all experience failure at one time or another in our lives. As actor Mickey Rooney put it, "You always pass failure on your way to success." Remember also that failure is an *event* or *situation* you find yourself in. You're in danger only when you begin describing *yourself* as the failure.

What are some steps you can take when life has handed you lemons and you haven't yet figured out how to make lemonade?

Be patient. This is a time of change, and things need to happen of their own accord. There is little to be gained by trying to speed up the process. If it takes you longer to get where you want to go, there might be a reason for it. It is often hard to figure out the big question "Why is this happening to me?" when you're in the middle of the crisis. Allow for Divine Wisdom to play a role in your life.

Have fun. When you're out of work, broke, and down on your luck, having fun may be at the bottom of your priority list. Nudge it up closer to the top. Come up with a list of inexpensive things you could do to enjoy yourself. There is no virtue in suffering needlessly while you're going through a difficult time.

Ask for help and guidance. If you open up and talk about what you're experiencing, you may be surprised by how many friends you have who want to help. You don't have to go through this alone. But if times are really tough or you feel you may be getting seriously depressed, be sure to talk with a therapist or your medical doctor.

Be gentle with yourself. Now is not the time to beat yourself up for any perceived mistakes or to wallow in "what I should have done." One of the biggest challenges most experience in the face of failure is knowing how to love ourselves through the process. Keep your heart and mind open and you'll find that insight and wisdom will come through when you most need them to guide you in the right direction.

*One must be a god to be able to tell successes
from failures without making a mistake.*

ANTON PAVLOVICH CHEKHOV

Practice positive self-talk. Remember that your thoughts direct the outcome of your life. Make sure you're headed in the right direction! Try out one or more of the following when you're feeling down or make up one of your own. You'll feel better fast.

I have what it takes to succeed.

Something better will come along.

I can relax into the flow of life and trust that things will get better.

Everything has a way of working out.

I've gotten through tough times before. I'll succeed again.

Life has a way of unfolding exactly as it should.

Chances are you've experienced a prior setback or challenge in your life. Bring it to mind and write a few sentences about it in your journal.

What do you remember about that time?

What were two or three things that helped get you through it?

What happened that ended that period of crisis?

What did you learn about yourself during that time?

Do you wish the event never took place or can you see the value of it from the position of hindsight?

The television minister and author Robert H. Schuller wrote a book called *Tough Times Never Last, but Tough People Do!* It's full of wonderful anecdotes and will make you feel better just knowing other people have walked through the valley and not only survived but flourished. I recommend it!

CHAPTER 26

Prosperity Is an Inside Job

Money is only an idea. If you want more money, simply change your thinking.

ROBERT T. KIYOSAKI

RON STARED IN DISBELIEF AT THE CHECK IN HIS HANDS. IT WAS FOR a hundred thousand dollars. Ron's uncle had died of cancer several months earlier and had left this amount for Ron. For years, Ron had dreamed about traveling, starting his own business, and buying a new truck. He had big dreams and yet always concluded he'd never be successful enough to make any kind of what he considered "big money." Now here he was with this check. It was more money than he had made in the past four years, and he was surprised to find he had very mixed feelings.

His first decision was to buy a new truck. He thought that this was a wise choice because he wanted to start a landscaping business. His friends kidded him, naming him "The King," but several of them called Ron and asked for "loans" of varying amounts. He felt uncomfortable because everyone began treating him a little differently and he didn't know whom to trust. He managed his uneasiness by buying extravagant gifts, giving away money, treating people to dinner, and leaving big tips.

Ron's girlfriend, Sarah, had always wanted to go on a vacation with him but they'd never done it because neither of them had any money. Ron decided this was their big chance and booked a lavish trip to Las Vegas. He thought Sarah would appreciate the gesture, but instead they fought constantly about money. Sarah was appalled at how fast Ron was spending his windfall and argued that he should at least put some of it aside until he could talk to a financial planner.

Over the next few months Ron spent his money extravagantly. In addition to the truck, he bought a new wardrobe and a bunch of electronic gadgets. He took flying lessons and purchased a small piece of land in a rural area several hours from his home. He made an attempt at starting a landscaping business but found he needed to invest in equipment and advertising in order to begin and his money was dwindling rapidly. He finally sought help from an accountant, who reminded Ron that he owed taxes on his inheritance. The amount was a little more than Ron had left in the bank. He sold a few of his now used toys, broke up with Sarah, and camped out on his piece of land for the summer. He was now worse off than he was before.

What happened? Ron's story, unfortunately, is not all that unusual. Research shows that many people who come into "instant money" through lotteries, inheritances, and insurance payouts mismanage their money and don't score significantly higher on "happiness tests" a year after their windfalls than they did before acquiring the money. Ron, like many others, had profound negative beliefs about money, his self-worth, and his ability to manage money. He also wasn't comfortable with the idea of having considerably more money than his friends.

Would you end up in the same situation as Ron if you were given a large amount of money? If you were honest with yourself you'd answer, "possibly." So how can you prepare yourself for the life of abundance you desire and deserve? First, you need to examine your beliefs about money.

Affirmations are much more than simple positive thinking. They are specific and powerful vehicles of change and if systematically employed, they can and do bring about such internal change, which, by consequence leads inevitably to external change.

JERROLD MUNDIS

Money, the lack of money, and people who *have* money are topics many of us have strong feelings about. There are four main areas in which our negative beliefs about money affect our lives in harmful ways. *Scarcity*—there isn't enough for me. *Money management*—I don't know what to do with money. *Rich people*—they're greedy, unjust, etc. And *self-worth*—I'm not good enough. Ron had almost all those beliefs and he created a situation in his life where he lost his entire inheritance in a little over a year because he made choices based on those erroneous beliefs.

One positive thought, when given a chance to take root and grow, can overpower an entire forest of negative thoughts. As you look at the list below, observe yourself and your own beliefs. Which of the negative statements resonate with you? Are they beliefs you hold? They may have served you in the past. They may not serve you now. Are you willing to change them?

Also look at the paragraph headed "Prospering Beliefs," which follows each list of Scarcity Thoughts. These are not meant to be an exhaustive list of possibilities but to offer another way of thinking about money, wealth, self-worth, and managing money. As you read the words, use your intuition. Find that peaceful-feeling place in yourself that resonates with the belief(s) you want to accept. As you look at the list of Prospering Beliefs, ask yourself, "Which of these thoughts feels better?"

Scarcity Thoughts:

I'll never get ahead.

I'll always be in debt.

I'll never have enough money.

I don't know how I'll be able to make more money.

If I have money, there won't be enough for others.

Your own ___

Prospering Beliefs:

It's okay to have money. There's more than enough to go around. I live in an abundant universe. I may have had difficulty with money in the past. This does not mean I need to continue to create this issue in the future. I am open and receptive to new avenues of abundance. I know that money and prosperity can come from a variety of sources. I trust that as I become clear about deserving money, it will begin to flow more abundantly in my life. I am becoming aware of my thoughts on this topic and consciously choosing to focus on what I want, rather than what I fear. God is working through me to help me develop a healthy attitude toward money. I choose to create prosperity in my life.

Money Management Issues:

I'm just not good with money.

I don't balance my checkbook.

I have no idea how much money I have (or don't have).

If I have money, I spend it.

Learning about investment strategies bores (or over-whelms) me.

Your own ___

Prospering Beliefs:

I choose to create a financial spending plan that works for me. I can easily ask for help and find the support that is most valuable to me. I affirm that I am capable of creating order in my financial affairs. My income continues to rise and I know how to manage this increase wisely. I enjoy spending money and saving money in a responsible manner. I am open to friends and mentors who can appropriately guide me to financial balance. I am not my debts. I choose to be both optimistic and practical about changing my financial life. I am beginning to learn about managing money. I find that the financial information is helpful and motivating especially if I take it a small step at a time. Every little bit of information helps me in my resolve to become financially secure. I am open to this guidance and act on its wisdom.

He that is discontented in one place
will seldom be content in another.

AESOP

People Who Are Wealthy:

Rich people aren't concerned about the poor and needy.

It's more spiritual to be poor.

Rich people don't care about others.

People who are wealthy are greedy (corrupt, dishonest . . .).

Rich people buy more stuff that pollutes the environment.

Your own ___

Prospering Beliefs:

It's okay to have money. It's okay to be wealthy and have more than enough money. Like most things in life, money can be used for good or bad purposes. I choose to focus my thoughts on all the good I can do with money. I release all anger, resentment, and blame. I know that there is enough abundance for everyone.

The more I have the more I can share with others. I enjoy using my money to educate and inform people about issues and causes I feel strongly about. Many wealthy people take great pleasure in being able to use their prosperity for good by using their funds for humanitarian work. I look forward to the time that I can do that as well. The Universe is filled with hope, joy, and enough for all.

Money Concerns:

I don't have what it takes to be successful.

You have to have money to make money.

I don't have enough (or the right) education.

I don't come from money.

Success happens to other people, not me.

Your own ___

Prospering Beliefs:

When I change my beliefs, I can change my life. I know that I create my own reality about money. I ask the Universe for help and understanding as I begin to change my money ideas to a more positive model. The past is over. I can be as successful as I make up my mind to be. My point of power is right *now*. I am able and willing to create success in my life, despite any difficult past life experiences. Everything about my life is beginning to work better and better. I see evidence of success in everything I do. I believe that golden opportunities abound!

The Universe always says yes. Pay attention to your thoughts, beliefs, and emotions. Figure out what the Universe is saying yes to! Do you want it to affirm that "Yes. I don't have enough money and never will"? Or do you want the Universe to say yes to the following: "I am worthy of abundance. I am somebody. I am worthy of a comfortable home, food on the table, and clothes for my family. I am open to all sources of abundance. I appreciate the wealth that comes to me through doing work I love. I have more than enough to meet my needs. I have financial security now and in the future." Amen.

CHAPTER 27

Make Your Vocation Your Vacation

When people go to work, they shouldn't have to leave their hearts at home.

BETTY BENDER

I'VE ALWAYS ENVIED THOSE PEOPLE WHO KNEW EXACTLY WHAT they wanted to be when they grew up. There were kids in my high school class who knew they were destined to have careers as veterinarians, accountants, nurses, or lawyers. I think those folks are rare. Most of us struggle with this question throughout our lives. We try to come up with a specific occupation that will satisfy all our needs at all stages of our life.

But what's not so rare is knowing what we're drawn to. It's almost as if there were a blueprint somewhere deep in our souls that lays out the best plan for our unfolding. It might be an interest that causes us to read any and all books on a certain topic. It could be a hobby we do in our spare time. Our calling might present itself as an issue we feel passionately about. As surprising as it may seem, most of us have a pretty good sense of our passion when we're children. We've just forgotten it and gone ahead and done things that are practical, logical, and rational with our lives. It's as if, like the Bender quote above states, "We've left our hearts at home."

The historian Arnold Toynbee once noted, "The supreme accomplishment is to blur the line between work and play." Yet most of us make choices based on family expectations, the current job market, or whatever is offered to us that enables us to pay the bills. We tune out the yearnings of our soul that call us to do the thing we're here to do. We convince ourselves we don't know what we want and even if we did have a clear sense, we believe we don't know how to get from here to there.

I was having dinner with some friends this past weekend. We were all self-employed and discussing the fact that what we were doing as adults were offshoots of what we loved to do as children. Carol talked about her love for music and movement. She had become a successful yoga teacher who used music to aid her students. She also loves learning about and attending operas in her free time. Joseph spoke about growing up in a small town. He developed mini-businesses such as lemonade stands, selling magazines, and trading baseball cards. He intuitively knew how to market things. He also loved writing short stories. He became a successful creative director at an advertising agency. We went around the table and each one there could see how his or her interests as a child and young adult fueled a successful career choice as each person grew older.

Our job is usually our main source of income and the vast majority of us spend at least half of our waking hours at this occupation. To say that it's important to enjoy the work you do is an understatement. Former President Theodore Roosevelt stated, "Far and away the best prize that life has to offer is the chance to work hard at work worth doing." How do you discover the vocation that makes you look forward to starting the day and makes the time fly by when you're doing it? Depending on which research study you read, anywhere from 40 percent to 60 percent of us don't like our current work. That's an awful lot of wasted time, energy, and talent.

To find joy in work is to discover the fountain of youth.

PEARL S. BUCK

Most people ask the wrong questions. The answer to "How can I make the most money?" may result in a career you despise that no amount of income would improve. Asking "What job could I choose that I'd be happy with for the rest of my life?" doesn't take into account the fact that you're likely to have changing needs, interests, and desires over the course of a lifetime of work.

Understandably, you want quick, surefire answers to your career-associated questions. However, intuition often guides you one step at a time. Ask your intuition the following questions and see what response ensues:

• How could I make money doing work I love?

• What kind of work do I feel excited about right now?

- What next step could I take to become clear about my career objectives?

- What kind of work would be most rewarding as I envision the next several years?

I've often joked that I wish we were born with a little instruction guide that, if followed, would lead to a successful life. It took me many years to understand that, in fact, intuition was that guide I was seeking. Instead of written instructions, God provided His wise direction for our calling to come through our still, quiet inner voice.

When I was in my mid-twenties I worked as the administrative director of Interface, a holistic education center near Boston. Many of the well-known self-help authors came there to give lectures and weekend seminars. I handled the logistics and programming details for Bernie Siegel, Deepak Chopra, Wayne Dyer, Christiane Northrup, Caroline Myss, and many others. Meeting them and hearing their talks fostered a strong desire in me to do something similar and yet, at the time, those luminaries seemed to be doing work far beyond my reach.

It took me eight years before I taught my first workshop and then a decade after that before my first book came out. Last summer I was presenting my "Compass of the Soul" seminar at the Omega Conference Center in Rhinebeck, New York. Deepak Chopra happened to be teaching the same weekend and I ran into him in the faculty lunchroom. He was quite gracious and in the course of our conversation, he said, "I purchased your book in the bookstore. It's very beautiful." It was one of those "aha!" moments in my life when I realized I had accomplished something I had set out to do many years before.

There is order in the Universe. There was a wise part that knew Interface was a good place for me to work when I was in my twenties. Much of what I learned there provided the foundation for what was to come in my life. I remember complaining at the time about how little I was paid. Yet, being there, meeting the people I met, and being exposed to their ideas have produced such rich rewards both financially and spiritually.

Nothing is work unless you'd rather
be doing something else.

GEORGE HALAS

God has a plan for your life. That plan is rarely shown to you all at once. It takes patience, trust, and faith to allow the often-miraculous details to unfold. It's not unlike putting a giant jigsaw puzzle together. You may have fragments that are clear, but until the final pieces fall into place you can't see the larger picture.

It's time to put the pieces together. You were born with natural talents, skills, and interests. Your life has been about discovering them and using them for a larger purpose to enrich, inspire, and help others. There is a saying from Buddha: "Your work is to discover your work and then with all your heart to give yourself to it." That said, how can you discover your work?

Following are some questions to get you started. You might want to grab your journal and carve out a few hours over the next several weeks or months to really tune in to your intuition and allow it to guide you. There are no wrong answers. Some of the questions will call to you more than others. Respond to those first. Like the puzzle analogy above, don't try to figure out the larger picture for now. Use these questions as a starting point, and it will become clear to you. As you write, pay attention to any messages of "quiet excitement," peace, calm, or confidence. These are ways your intuition has of communicating something of importance.

- What did I love to do as a child?

- What do I like to read about or study in my free time?

- At the end of my life what will I be most proud of having accomplished?

- What am I doing when time flies by?

- What would I be doing if I didn't have to work for money?

- What quality do I possess that people most often comment on?

- What skill(s) do I possess that people most often comment on?

- What wrong would I most like to right in the world?

- If I had a precious secret to share with children that would help them be successful, what would that secret be?

- What would I do if I knew I'd succeed?

- If I had the perfect job or career, what would an ideal day, week, and month look like?

- What types of people would I like to work with?

- Do I want to be self-employed or work for a company and receive a paycheck?

- What would my best friend tell me I should do for work?

- When I tune in to my inner guidance, what does it tell me I should do?

*Through the grace of God we have different gifts.
If our gift is preaching, let us preach to the limit of our
vision. If it is serving others let us concentrate on our
service; if it is teaching let us give all that we have to
our teaching; and if our gift is stimulating the faith of
others let us set ourselves to it. Let the man who is called
to give, give freely; let the man in authority work with
enthusiasm; and let the man who feels sympathy for
his fellows in distress help them cheerfully.*

ROMANS 12: 6–8 (PHILLIPS TRANSLATION)

- How could I make a living doing what I love?

- What was I doing the last time I had fun?

- What's missing in my life and what could I do to supply the missing piece?

- What can I do this week (month, year) to take a step toward what I've learned in this exercise?

The Universe is a great teacher. People who have a sense of purpose and who follow their passion are rewarded with joy and energy and are fueled by inspiration. It's as if they are dancing with life and the Universe rewards the dancers with abundance in all forms. It's time to put on your dancing shoes, have fun, and kick up your heels! Dancing lessons, anyone?

CHAPTER 28

How to Grow a Life You Love

I could be whatever I wanted to be if I trusted that music,
that song, that vibration of God that was inside of me.

SHIRLEY MACLAINE

FAMILY CIRCLE MAGAZINE REPORTED THAT IN 1993, 83 PERCENT OF working adults described their jobs as satisfying. In 2003, the satisfaction rate had dropped to 54 percent. It's rather a shocking number. How would you answer the question about your job satisfaction? When you consider the percentage of time you spend each week being at work, commuting to work, thinking about work, and possibly doing your work at home, it's a huge portion of your life. Would you be in the group that didn't like its work?

Megan definitely fit the description of the job dissatisfaction category. She sat in my office and looked exhausted. "I hate my job. But I need it too, because it provides the money to pay the mortgage, the food, and the kids' education. I really want to start an event-planning business but I don't have time because I have to work." She continued complaining about her job, sinking more deeply into the couch she was sitting on before I stopped her.

I asked her to describe the event-planning business she had mentioned and she brightened. Her posture straightened, she smiled, and she looked directly at me for the first time since entering my office. She told me that ever since she was a kid, she'd enjoyed organizing parties. She loved creating special occasions for people, complete with entertainment, decorations, and themes. Her creative instincts were fully involved when envisioning and choreographing a successful event.

When I questioned her about why she wasn't beginning her business now since it gave her so much pleasure, she once again began her litany of complaints about not having enough time because of her job. "Do you think you'll be at this job forever?" I asked. She looked surprised and responded that her present company was merging with a larger firm and, in fact, her job future was uncertain. "That's great!" I replied. "Let's create a strategy for building a new work life for you." Following are some of the things we addressed in our sessions together:

Honor your intuition. Everybody has a calling in life. Part of your task is to discover this passion. It doesn't need to be an ostentatious thing and it's not a job description. It's the thing that makes you take pleasure in life. For some, like Megan, this part comes easily. She enjoys using her creative skills to help people have fun. She described it to me as "love personified." For others, no easy goal or ambition leaps to mind. I often hear people tell me about something they would love to do and then just as quickly dismiss it as "not possible." Begin to pay attention to those little flickers of enthusiasm. Don't let them go so easily. They are part of your inner guidance trying to give you some needed direction. Entertain the possibility that there is life beyond the drudgery of your current work. If *you* can't identify what you love, how can the Universe provide it for you?

I don't know much about being a millionaire,
but I'll bet I'd be a darling at it.

DOROTHY PARKER

Here are some questions to get you started. If you could retire comfortably right now, how would you spend your time? Another way of thinking about this is, if you won the lottery this month, what would you do with the money once you got past the phase of buying a new house, taking some trips, donating to charity, and paying the bills? Reach beyond the obvious and spend some time on these questions and begin to envision a life where you could do what you love. Even multimillionaires find the need to do something with their time, talents, and passions!

Don't overlook your present job. Once you've identified what you love to do, is there a way to do it—at least some of it—where you currently work? For example, it had never occurred to Megan that her present firm might need her services as a meeting planner. While it wasn't part of her current job description, she sought out the person in the company who handled many of the larger meeting logistics and asked how she could help.

The Universe often responds with amazing synchronicity when you identify your needs. The woman whom Megan spoke with was pregnant. She had just begun to think about the details of how to manage the transition of her job while she was on maternity leave. Megan showed up at the right place at the right time in order to help her. In fact, it turned out even better. After the woman came back from her leave, all involved decided that Megan should continue the meeting planning and it became a larger part of her job description.

Consider self-employment. It's important to both listen to your intuition when it indicates it's time for a change, and yet be practical enough that you don't create a crisis by leaving a job prematurely. Megan eventually wanted to work for herself but was delighted that she could gain needed experience and contacts while remaining a full-time employee. We discussed a plan further down the road where she could honor her inner desire to be an entrepreneur.

Most people don't have the necessary financial reserves to simply decide that they can leave their full-time job and begin to work for themselves. If that's true for you, what are some other ways that you can make the transition? Think about using your evenings, weekends, and/or vacation for a certain period of time to begin your self-employment work. This gives you the opportunity to build a client base while still receiving a regular paycheck and benefits from your full-time work.

In the current economy, many are choosing to work several jobs on a part-time basis. The downside is that it's difficult to find part-time positions that have health insurance and other benefits. However, for some, this is not a significant disadvantage and they relish the autonomy and flexibility that part-time work entails. If you're thinking of leaving a permanent full-time job to go out on your own, find out first if your employer would consider having you stay on in a part-time capacity. This may be a win-win for all involved.

Is volunteering an option? If you're not inspired by the thought of being an entrepreneur and you don't want to look for another job right now, perhaps your current work situation would feel more satisfactory if you had another outlet for your interests and talents. What could you do in your free time that would feel like fun and allow you to make a contribution? If you're stuck for ideas, many communities have "voluntary action centers" coordinated through nonprofit organizations. Or look for "volunteer wanted" listings in the local newspaper.

There is no paycheck that can equal the feeling
of contentment that comes from being
the person you are meant to be.

OPRAH WINFREY

I've had clients come up with a wide range of activities from walking dogs at the local humane society, to helping nursing home residents style their hair, to working with teenagers in a local theater troupe. People report that their volunteer work created new relationships and community and allowed them to see themselves in a fresh and vibrant way. Better yet, volunteer work has opened the door for many to get paid for what they love. Think about it. When you're doing activities you enjoy, you're in a milieu that puts you in contact with other people who have similar interests. What better way for the Universe to work its magic than to put you in contact with just the right person with just the right job for you at just the right salary? You may need to take the first step toward the work you love by volunteering and allow God to do the rest.

Manage your time more effectively. Sometimes it's hard to make room for prosperity-producing intuitive information to flow in because your life and mind are already filled to the brim. Certainly it's difficult to imagine actually making a change to add something new and wonderful to your life when you are already too busy. Megan admitted that she was one of those people who felt she needed a life balance makeover. She claimed she wanted more quality time for her husband and kids, more time for herself and her spiritual life, as well as more time to see her friends. However, these priorities were not reflected in how she managed her time.

I asked her to think about her life and identify the situations that drained her or took her energy. We looked at her schedule and noted the most stressful times of each day. Getting the kids off to school each morning and managing the chaos around dinnertime and homework were the top areas she wanted to change. She also spoke about a friend who called every day and took a lot of her energy. Megan described their connection as an "ain't life awful" relationship and she wanted to change it to one that was more positive for both of them.

Your intuition gives you information in two very basic ways. When you're drained by something, that's your inner guidance steering you away from that person or situation. Reflecting on that, what change is your intuition indicating in your life? What can you let go of in order to make room for the new and wonderful life you so richly deserve? Conversely, when you feel a sense of enthusiasm around the idea of pursuing something, that's your intuition saying yes!

Begin to trust your "inner compass" to lead you in the right direction. It takes willingness on your part to do the hard work of asking questions and staying open to the answers. It also requires a readiness to take risks and move out of your comfort zone.

CHAPTER 29

Dear God: Send Money

We can loan you enough money to get you completely out of debt.

SIGN ON BANK

YOU'VE BEEN FIRED OR LAID OFF. YOUR CHILD IS SICK AND YOU don't have insurance. Your spouse has been in an accident and is out of work. Your furnace decided to quit in the middle of a cold winter and they're telling you it needs to be replaced. All you know is that you're scared and you need money fast. You start worrying incessantly. Panic sets in. You have visions of losing the house and debt collectors calling at all hours. How will you survive? Where can you find the money?

Okay. Stop. Slow down. There is a way. And panic, worry, and fear are not good places to start. It only impedes the flow of the very abundance you seek. If you find yourself in a desperate financial circumstance and need to change things fast, here are some ways to get through it.

Prosperity key #1: Stay focused in the present.

It's hard not to feel panicked when your mind is painting vivid pictures of situations that you fear *may* befall you. A missed mortgage payment may have your mind racing with thoughts of losing your home and being out on the street. Right now you're okay and your Divine intuition is already kicking in to give you some much needed help. Whenever you find yourself experiencing fearful thoughts about the future, bring yourself back to the present. Keep your thoughts focused on right now. Your task is to stay calm and present so you can be open to the flow of both wise guidance and Divine prosperity.

Prosperity key #2: Get clear what you want.

Write a list of what you need right now. Don't try to figure out *how* these things will come to you. Allow the Universe to do what it does best—create miracles. Your highly charged emotional thoughts create what you draw to you. Keep your focus on what you want, not on what you don't want. Maintain an attitude of surrender about *how* these things, or this money, will come to you. The Universe has been known to create minor miracles such as causing the sun to come up every morning and to go down every night. Perhaps you might allow it to help you create an answer to your personal needs right now?

Prosperity key #3: Stop worrying.

Worry is a choice and it's always counterproductive. When you catch yourself doing it, shift your focus. Worrying about money does not bring more money into your life. (If only that were true, we'd all be rich!) Worrying will not bring one more dollar to you. In fact, the opposite is true. When you have faith and an attitude of trust, you're more open and receptive to the thoughts, feelings, and impulses from the Universe that direct you toward true prosperity. The more you think about something, the more you bring it about. Worry interferes with your hopes, dreams, and desires. If it's difficult for you to stop worrying, try taking it a day at a time. Tell yourself, "Today [or this moment] I'm choosing not to worry."

Prosperity key #4: Brainstorm some possibilities.

Get a paper and pen or put fingers to your keyboard and begin writing down every possible solution that pops into your mind. Do this once a day for thirty days. Ask your intuition questions as you write: "How can I create immediate cash right now?" "What's the best course of action to help me ___?" (Fill in the blank.) "What can I do that would be most helpful for me right now?" If you're feeling stuck, call some supportive friends and invite them to a potluck meal and prosperity-brainstorming party. The more creative the ideas, the merrier!

Prosperity key #5: Take action on the answers you receive.

It's easy to feel paralyzed when crisis strikes. Don't overwhelm yourself. Break the tasks down so that you're taking at least two action steps a day. If more steps feel comfortable to you, that's fine too. You are putting out energy toward what you want to create. Take action only on those items that feel life-giving and energizing. If you feel drained and enervated when contemplating an action, don't do it. Those responses are your intuition at work, pointing you in the right direction. Keep a journal of each task that you've completed, including some of the less tangible ones in this chapter. There's something very comforting in seeing a list of accomplishments when you're down on yourself and feel that you're not "doing enough."

Prosperity key #6: Watch for miracles to occur.

Know that you're in the process of creating a solution to your crisis. The Universe is on your side. You're not alone. The answer may not come all at once. Begin to look for evidence that things are turning around for you. Perhaps an unexpected source of money comes to you, or you have an interview for a new job. Maybe the car repair that you thought was going to cost you hundreds of dollars only costs you a fraction of that. Write about these occasions in your journal and look at them frequently.

Let go of your fear. The universe has an infinite
supply of opportunity. There is plenty to go around.
You may be surprised to see that something
is coming your way right now.

RICHARD CARLSON

Prosperity key #7: Stay open to God's abundance.

Your role is to *allow* the abundance to come into your life. The way you disallow it is through fear and worry. The way to let it in is by having faith, staying happy, and keeping your mind and heart open. In the Talmud it says: "In the world to come each of us will be called to account for all the good things God put on this earth which we refused to enjoy." Open your heart to God and let Him know about your fears, concerns, hopes, and dreams. Talk to Him as if He were a friend. Ask for inspiration, faith, confidence, and abundance.

Prosperity key #8: Slow down.

In the midst of a crisis it's all too easy to endlessly focus on the chaos around you. Money and other forms of abundance do not necessarily come more quickly to you when you're in a frenzied state. In fact the opposite is true. Take five minutes each morning, afternoon, and evening for at least a thirty-day period to simply sit and breathe. You'll be surprised how this one act will make you feel more centered and thus more open to abundance.

Prosperity key #9: Make a commitment to stay positive.

We all have habits of unconstructive thoughts that we repeat to ourselves when we're under pressure. What thoughts do you have? A common one I hear people say is, "I'm so stressed out!" Be vigilant about nipping those negative thought spirals in the bud. Pessimistic thinking often precedes an emotional crash and you can't afford one of those when you're in a financial crisis. Following are some prosperity-affirming thoughts that will help you stay positive. Pick one that works for you. The intention is to make you feel better so you can stay open to incoming intuitive guidance that will lead you out of the current situation. "This is just temporary. Things are beginning to turn around." "I am open to new avenues of prosperity." "I live in an abundant Universe. I have everything I need." "Money flows to me from all directions." Write down several statements that make you feel better and replace those nasty negative thoughts with some good ones.

Prosperity key #10: Keep a gratitude journal.

Gratitude is the stuff prosperity is made of. There is no better time than when you're in the midst of a crisis to begin or maintain a journal filled with appreciation. What you focus on expands. Find delicious moments throughout the day and savor their power. Did your child say something sweet to you today? Did you receive an unexpected check in the mail? Perhaps you took a walk and your neighbors stopped to chat. Or you unexpectedly felt thankful for a clear mind and healthy body. Every night before you go to bed, write down at least six things that were wonderful today.

---

*The trouble with having your money work for you
is that sometimes it gets fired.*

JERRY SEINFELD

Prosperity key #11: Allow yourself time to dream.

It's often difficult to imagine a healthy, balanced, prosperous, and successful life when you're feeling scared and things around you are in disarray. However, this is the time when it's most important. Actively visualize what you want to create in your new reality. Get out your journal, your set of paints, or your colored pens and begin to write down and draw images of what you want your life to become. If you're not particularly creative, get a stack of magazines and cut out pictures of what you want. Put these images and words in a place where you'll feel inspired.

Prosperity key #12: Take prosperity meditation breaks.

You don't need to sneak away from your desk or even take long periods of time for this to work. Think of these as thirty-second abundance contemplations. Simply allow your thoughts to open to abundance. As you do this, expand your feelings to include a sense of safety, faith, and love. Are there any images or emotions that come to mind that allow you to feel more abundant? If so, expand or pump up the volume of those feelings.

Prosperity key #13: Talk to supportive friends and colleagues.

Haven't you felt good in the past when someone close to you allowed you to be helpful and supportive? Allow people around you to do the same. The Universe often creates miracles through our connections to others. Let them know what's going on with you. Your friends often don't know what you need or the kind of support you find most helpful. So ask for what you want. They may have just the right contact, advice, or information that will relieve or solve your problems.

Prosperity key #14: Acknowledge the abundance you already have.

Make a point of looking around you throughout the day and consciously focusing on the plenty that exists. Take a walk and breathe in the air. No lack there! Depending on where you live and what season it is, take in the profusion of sand, snow, leaves, trees, or grass that fill your surroundings. Go to a grocery store and marvel at the large quantity of fruits and vegetables. And don't overlook the less tangible things like the fact that you may have wonderful friends, a good job, and/or a healthy body. Your intention here is to keep your focus off the illusion of lack and on the reality of true abundance. Every time you appreciate the wealth that exists in you and around you, you are reminding yourself that you are on a planet that is chock full of everything you need.

Prosperity key #15: Have compassion for yourself.

We all mess up from time to time. Don't allow a temporary crisis with your finances to be another occasion to beat yourself up. Think about some creative ways to experience self-nurturing during this difficult time. What are some affordable luxuries you could treat yourself to so you don't feel totally deprived? You could buy some delicious gourmet jam to use on your morning toast; a new color of polish to brighten your nails; or reward yourself by going out for a bowl of soup at a local restaurant. There are less tangible things you can do that are helpful during times of stress. Making sure you get enough sleep is an obvious one, but also simply taking time to read a book or watch a good movie can help get your mind off your concerns. Often all it takes are very simple shifts of attitude to invite prosperity into your life. Loving yourself opens the path for more love—and prosperity—from the Universe.

CHAPTER 30

The Cycle of Abundance

Divine love in and through me, blesses and multiplies
the awareness of all the good that I have, all the good
that I give, and all the good that I receive.

UNITY CHURCH PRAYER

I ATTENDED COLLEGE IN A SMALL TOWN IN SOUTHERN VERMONT.
As part of my curriculum I was required to create a project that
would enhance the community in some way. I had worked in
several nonprofit social service organizations at that stage in my
life and recognized the value and importance of volunteers. I
also knew that the average person had no idea about many of
those opportunities. I decided my school project was to create a
"volunteer clearinghouse" for my area.

I set up meetings with fifteen social service agencies. I asked
them about their needs for volunteers and created a "job description" for each position. After compiling a list, I advertised in the
local paper and created a public service announcement that aired

on two radio stations. I was swamped with replies; people wanted to give back.

I interviewed all the volunteers who applied and was truly inspired by the love and caring that people had for others in their community. Many said that they just hadn't been aware of how to channel their desire to help. "I don't have a lot of money, but I have a lot of love," said one older woman, who decided to spend several hours a week at a local day care. A man who had retired from his work as a home builder volunteered his time to the Big Brothers organization and helped his "little brother" learn carpentry skills. Another woman offered to read each week to several young girls who were being helped by the local association for the blind.

At the end of a six-month period my college program required that I assess the success of the school project. To accomplish that, I interviewed the volunteers. Every single person told me they received so much more than they gave. "I feel rich in friends and community," said one. "My heart feels open. The kids' eyes light up when I walk into the room. It makes me feel alive again." Others reported their choice of assignment had opened the door for a new career direction, gave them self-confidence, boosted their self-esteem, and enriched their lives immeasurably. The comment I heard most often was, "I received so much more than I gave."

Part of living a life of true prosperity is to understand that giving and receiving are vital forms of the same Universal energy. If you simply take without giving, you are stopping the flow. A prosperous person is someone who gives back whether it's through a donation of time, money, or ideas, or through some other means. By giving of what you have, you also allow more to flow through you and your life. American inventor R. G. LeTourneau humorously stated, "I shovel [money] out, and God shovels it back . . . but God has a bigger shovel!"

You live in a bountiful universe. You can tap into that powerful force through your own generosity. Prosperity is about flow. When you align with God, you bless others and give of your time and talents. Doing so creates a magnetic energy that will attract even more money, ideas, and prospering circumstances to you.

We make a living by what we get;
we make a life by what we give.

WINSTON CHURCHILL

Don't just give money; give your time and ideas as well. I mentioned at the beginning of the chapter that volunteering is a wonderful way to give back to the community by making a gift of yourself. What are you good at? What do you love to do? You've invested in yourself in ways that enabled you to learn a skill or develop a talent. Whom can you share it with?

Try an experiment. If you begin to feel that you lack something in your life, give part of what you have to someone else. If you're feeling financially poor, give a small donation to a charity, or a larger tip than usual to the waitress who serves you your morning coffee. Send a silent blessing to strangers you pass on the way to work. Give to the homeless person on the street. Offer to do a small kindness for a neighbor. Call someone on the phone or send a card when you know the person needs a boost. Giving affirms your true prosperity. It strengthens your connection to others. It allows abundance to flow from you to others and back again.

I received a note from one of my newsletter subscribers. She wrote, "I have found that what goes around comes around. I love to give, whether it's money, actual items (like a meal at Thanksgiving) or my time. When I give, I receive. I don't *always* get money or material things, but often when I'm feeling lonely, a simple phone call from a friend arrives to cheer my day."

Philanthropist Robert B. Pamplin, Jr., encourages generosity by saying, "Every time we give a gift, we are adding something profound to the world—passing along something entirely intangible, a pure emotion—to a fellow traveler. This sort of gift requires that the heart and mind work together; it springs from the center of the soul, from pure caring and love. It's the best thing we can do as humans—not because we have to, but because we want to."

Most of the time when we think of giving, we think of money. Tithing is a term familiar to almost every religion in the world. The word *tithe* literally means a "tenth." To tithe means to give back 10 percent of your gross earnings to the place where you receive your spiritual sustenance. In the past, people have given to their mosque, temple, church, or ashram. American industrialist and philanthropist John D. Rockefeller, Sr., was firmly committed to the concept of tithing, saying, "I never would have been able to tithe the first million dollars I ever made if I had not tithed my first salary, which was $1.50 per week."

That statement is enough to give you hope for your own prosperity!

Tithing to one's place of worship is still practiced by many. However, others have expanded the definition of where one receives spiritual sustenance and have concluded that many things can feed your soul. I have clients who gave to individuals and organizations that provide uplifting music, beautiful art, spiritual literature, caretaking of the environment, and help for those in need in their community.

From abundance he took abundance,
and still abundance remained.

THE UPANISHADS

Giving 10 percent of your income can be a bit scary at first. Would you be willing to start with just 2 percent? If you're making $25,000 a year, 2 percent is $41.66 a month or about $1.40 a day. Think of how good it feels to open your heart to give. Even if you're currently experiencing debt, consider donating just $5.00 a month to a worthy cause of your choice. Several of my clients have found it helpful to not only keep track of their contributions but to keep track of the benefits they've *received* from their gifts as well. Many who have begun to tithe regularly report unexpected amounts of money, opportunities, and ideas suddenly coming into their lives in seemingly miraculous ways.

The minister John Wesley exhorts us to "Earn as much as you can. Save as much as you can. Invest as much as you can. Give as much as you can." Giving makes me feel prosperous. I send each check with a silent blessing. "Thank you, God, for the ample abundance in my life. I know that as I write this check it goes to bless the receiver and returns to me multiplied." I then close with a specific prayer for the person or organization to which the money is being sent. I like to think of my donation as adding to "The Universal Mutual Fund."

What does giving do? It:

Reminds you to be grateful.

Connects you with your Source.

Opens new channels to abundance.

Builds your self-confidence.

Allows you to empower others.

Permits you to enrich organizations you support.

Circulates the flow of abundance in the world.

Returns to you multiplied.

Allows new opportunities to come into your life.

Revitalizes your community.

Enlarges your ability to give even more abundantly.

Demonstrates your belief in your own prosperity.

Establishes confidence in an abundant universe.

Increases your ability to give more.

Prosperity, love, and abundance circulate throughout our world and through all our lives. There is a never-ending current of giving and receiving. When you give your money, time, and kindness, you open yourself to receiving it back multiplied. Giving—all by itself—creates riches. The Universe is abundant. There is more than enough for all. We were placed here to live our lives as a full expression of God. Enjoy your journey and may you continue to prosper for all the days of your life.

Products and Services for Success

Lectures and Seminars

Are you looking for a dynamic, inspiring, entertaining, and informative speaker for your next conference or corporate event? Lynn Robinson is one of the nation's leading experts on the topic of intuition. She is also one of the best speakers on the subject. A member of the National Speakers Association with more than fifteen years of speaking experience, Lynn consistently receives rave reviews for the depth of her content, the good-natured, down-to-earth style in which she delivers it, and her winning sense of humor.

Intuitive Consulting for Business

Could your business use an edge? Many business decisions need to be made quickly. Logic and analysis can provide only partial answers, and often there is inadequate data on which to base a decision. Lynn uses her intuition to tune in to the core of your business challenge. The insights she gets can help you create solutions that enable you to achieve your goals quickly and effectively.

Her insights cover a wide spectrum, including creative marketing strategies, ways to build employee motivation, improving the odds on an important sales pitch, and much more.

Personal Consultations

Consultations with Lynn have a powerful blend of psychology, metaphysics, and spirituality combined with her background in business and marketing. Her work is not based on detailed predictions because she believes we have a great deal of free will in determining our future. Lynn assists you through a combination of insightful questions and intuitive guidance. The session will help you identify your goals and show you the path that will take you there.

Audiotapes and CDs

Lynn's guided imagery tapes include "The Intuitive Life Series," "Prosperity! The Intuitive Path to Creating Abundance," "Creating the Life You Want," and many others. Lynn has also put two of her classes on CD. "Creative Marketing for Entrepreneurs" and "The Intuitive Path to Prosperity!" Each class is one hour in length.

Free E-mail Intuition Newsletter

You'll receive a monthly e-mail digest packed with information you can use, including valuable tips on how to develop your intuition, reviews of interesting and relevant books, plus intuition and spirituality-related Web links. You can sign up for this through Lynn's Web site.

About the Author

LYNN ROBINSON, M.ED., IS RECOGNIZED AS ONE OF THE NATION'S leading experts on intuition. She is a best-selling author, consultant, and sought-after motivational speaker who teaches that when we know how to access its enormous power, the remarkable benefits of intuition are available to us all.

Lynn has used her intuition to help thousands of people create success in life and business. She often works directly with corporations on projects that include new business initiatives, mergers and acquisitions, marketing, executive hiring, and introducing new products such as the Schick Intuition razor for women.

She has been featured in *USA Today,* interviewed by the *New York Times,* been a guest on many popular radio and television programs, and is currently the Intuition-At-Work Expert for iVillage.com.

She has been a professional intuitive since 1983 and is founder and president of Intuitive Consulting Inc.

Contact Information

Lynn A. Robinson
Intuitive Consulting Inc.
P.O. Box 81218
Wellesley Hills, Massachusetts 02481

800-925-4002 or 617-964-0075

E-mail: Lynn@LynnRobinson.com

Web site: http://www.LynnRobinson.com